Tuisco Greiner
A Man Redeemed

Donna J. Wells

"But it is with soils as it is with people when they get in a bad way. If the foundation – the texture, the quality, the character is good, they can be redeemed very easily."

Tuisco Greiner The Garden Book For Practical Farmers Vol. 2 (1901)

"The LORD redeems the soul of his servants.
And none of those who trust in him shall be condemned."

Psalm 34: 23

ISBN 978-1-64191-423-9 (paperback)
ISBN 978-1-64191-424-6 (digital)

Copyright © 2018 by Donna J. Wells

All rights reserved. No part of this publication may be reproduced, distributed, or transmitted in any form or by any means, including photocopying, recording, or other electronic or mechanical methods without the prior written permission of the publisher. For permission requests, solicit the publisher via the address below.

Christian Faith Publishing, Inc.
832 Park Avenue
Meadville, PA 16335
www.christianfaithpublishing.com

Printed in the United States of America

In Memory of

Claudia Göbig Wells
1962-2012

She lived, loved and laughed with all her heart,
and left us too soon.

Acknowledgements

Tuisco Greiner, A Man Redeemed, is purely a labor of love, not only for all those who appreciate the foundations that our ancestors built for each one of us, but, especially for my family.

Thank you for believing in me, for correcting my mistakes and for patiently listening to me when my excitement bubbled over every time I found something new and interesting about our ancestors!

Thank you, my sister Cora for believing in me, praying for me, and proofreading for me - and my brother Jeff for being in the right place at the right time, to find our Greiner family in Germany.

Thank you, cousins Dave Olney, great-grandson of Friedemann Greiner, and Jose Luis Greiner, grandson of Tuisco Greiner, for providing many of the pictures for this book.

I also want to include a special thank-you to Tom Tryniski, for scanning thousands of New York State Newspapers – and making them searchable online, because this book could never have been written without the multitude of newspaper articles that tell the stories no one in the family would, or could tell, about Tuisco Greiner.

Helma Greiner Merrill
1905-2001

This book is dedicated to my Grandmother, Helma Greiner Merrill who, like her father, Tuisco Greiner, spent her life teaching. She taught school children, her own children, her grandchildren and even some great-grandchildren. She taught me to work hard, to keep a spotless house and to cook the best meals ever! She taught me how to take care of little ones when she put me to bed at night – my head between the pillows, and the fresh, crisply ironed, white sheets so tightly tucked around me that I couldn't possibly fall out! She always gave us her best, whether it was a big hug, or a good scolding - as needed!

I wish I could say I do all of that as well as she did, but I fall far short of her example, although I did manage to make a batch of bread and butter pickles every bit as good as hers… but only once.

The most important thing she taught me, just by the way she lived her life, was that God and family matter.

I was very young the day she introduced me to church, and to the awesome, reverent peace I felt, just being there. And I remember the day she opened the crumbling velvet covered picture album to show me her parents, Tuisco and Cora Bartholomew Greiner. Both of them had died when she was just nine years old.

In introducing me to my great-grandparents, she not only taught me how precious family is, she sparked in me a curiosity to know more. She taught me who I am.

Contents

Preface 1
Introduction 5
Chapter One: Meeting the Greiners 7
Chapter Two: The Immigrant's Parents 15
Chapter Three: The Immigrants 19
Chapter Four: Golden Years of Garlinghouse 25
Chapter Five: A Booming Business 31
Chapter Six: "The Change" 41
Chapter Seven: A Time to Forgive 51
Chapter Eight: La Salle and Family Life 55
Chapter Nine: The "Doughty Reformer" 63
Chapter Ten: Heartbreak and Tragedy 74
Chapter Eleven: Life Is What You Make of It 102
Chapter Twelve: For Love of the Garden 107
Chapter Thirteen: An Opinionated Man 111
Chapter Fourteen: Benefits of a Proper Diet 122
Chapter Fifteen: The "Ingenious" Greiner Brothers 128

Chapter Sixteen: Getting to Know Karl Gotthold Greiner 134

Chapter Seventeen: Getting to Know Friedemann Greiner.........147

Chapter Eighteen: Tuisco, In Other's Words................................157

Chapter Nineteen: Goodbye… For Now....................................160

Chapter Twenty: "An All-Abiding Faith" 164

Chapter Twenty-One: The Name 167

Chapter Twenty-Two: Still Relevant 170

A Lovely Ending in a Shady Grove 181

Index of Names 183

Preface

Searching for the Real Tuisco Greiner

I had heard a few stories about my ancestors while I was growing up, but I didn't pay much attention. I was sure that none of them were very notable, in fact, I carelessly assumed that I was descended from a "long line of farmers", as I recall one relative saying. Honest, hardworking people. No one told stories about war heroes or anyone famous – at least none that I could remember. I do recall something about glassmaking, and a book about onions in the Library of Congress, but at such a young age, I suppose I thought it was just another story that grown-ups tell that really didn't have anything to do with me.

As I grew into adulthood, I worked at several different occupations until I was hired as a Customer Service Representative at a call center. I often worked late at night when the calls were few and far between. I thought I would go crazy if I didn't find something to keep me busy in-between calls.

I wracked my brain to find something interesting, but nothing hit the mark until I remembered the ads for ancestry.com. I had long felt an empty void where my roots should have been. Like one of Tuisco's plants, I felt that I couldn't really grow or progress until I discovered and nurtured those family roots. I needed to find out about the people who made me who I am. Good or bad - I wanted to know it all.

I was grateful that my employer allowed me to use the internet during slow times, and so I got started.

I found a lot of information on several ancestry websites, but it wasn't enough. Names, numbers and places were a good start, but I wanted to know more. What did they do? What did they think?

I tried a general search by typing in names, birth and death dates, which led me to googlebooks and numerous family websites. What I found was so amazing! There was so much more to my family history than I could ever have imagined! Among those discoveries, I found that there really is a connection to glassblowing, and more than just one book on vegetables in the Library of Congress with Tuisco Greiner's name on the cover.

He and two of his brothers, Karl Gotthold and Friedemann, separately immigrated to America from Germany. Gotthold arrived in 1862, Tuisco in 1869 and Friedemann in 1872. All three of them made quite an impression in their new homeland with their faith, hard work, industriousness and such a passion for their own crafts, that all three brothers felt compelled to share their knowledge, innovative ideas and experiments in trade magazines, newspaper articles, books and speeches. Gotthold and Friedemann became master beekeepers with extensive aviaries, and were active leaders in their local chapters of the National Bee Association.

Tuisco's occupations were a little more diverse. He was a market gardener, an experimental seed producer, seed store owner, an advocate for healthy diets, new and improved gardening and farming techniques. He was a politician and a popular author of numerous how-to books and magazine articles on innovative gardening practices that are still available through internet shopping sites, and are still being quoted in books and articles about gardening down to this day. He was also, as I would find, quite a character.

I discovered the *real* Tuisco Greiner – his faults and his glory, his thoughts and his character - not only in his books, in his own words, but in newspapers articles that chronicled his life in personal ways we might never have known if we only concentrated on matter-of-fact records.

Tom Tryniski had scanned thousands of New York State newspapers and posted them on his website, Fultonhistory.com. - a phenomenal accomplishment that professional and amateur genealogists will forever be grateful for!

I typed "Tuisco Greiner, Naples" into the search box, and article after article popped up in the results column. I eagerly devoured every one of those amazing articles! Some made me cry, some made me laugh – I was in awe of Tuisco and his brothers, Gotthold and Friedemann - their industriousness and success! I wondered how this simple farm girl could be related to them.

Then... it all changed. I started finding articles that shocked and confused me as I read things like:

"Debt, Deviltry, Desertion and Disgrace!"

"Saturday was a lively day on the street; the Greiner affair was the main cause."

"The Tuisco Greiner affair is the nine-day wonder of the town."

"The excitement on "the Change" this morning was great on account of the disappearance of Tuisco Greiner yesterday."

What? This couldn't be my great-grandfather – this must be the wrong Tuisco Greiner!

I checked and re-checked. It was indeed the Naples Record, and The Neapolitan, of Naples, NY, and it *was* indeed my own great-grandfather that was somehow crashing and burning before my eyes!

I had to know – *what happened!* Who was this man, really? Was he as bad as the town of Naples was making him out to be? I kept reading, and slowly the story of my great-Grandfather unfolded with each article, and I remembered all the mistakes I had made in my lifetime. Only then, was I able to look beyond the headlines and try to piece together the *real* story of Tuisco Greiner, an imperfect human being, and an amazing man from Bernburg, Germany.

A Man Redeemed.

INTRODUCTION

"People like to be amused. If I possessed the faculty of writing amusingly, I would put it to good use in writing this book. But an author who has no higher aim in writing anything, may this be a simple newspaper article or the most voluminous book, than to amuse, has missed his calling, and could render far greater service to the world by hoeing potatoes, or digging ditches than by wasting his opportunities and misusing pen and paper.

As I can not (sic) hope to amuse the reader, I shall at least try hard to interest him. This is only for a better purpose, however, and as a means to an end. I want to induce every one into whose hands this book may fall to read the following pages with care, and I give fair warning beforehand that it is my purpose to use every means in my power, short of actual deception and misrepresentation, every fact and every argument that I know of, and try to make my brother farmers see in the home garden all that I have found in it, to tell them how to get all the benefits out of it, and thus to lift some of the burdens now resting on their shoulders, and to add new comforts, new pleasures, and new profits to their calling."

Tuisco Greiner
Introduction to "The Garden Book for Practical Farmers" 1901

A Great-Granddaughter's Response

My sincere hope and prayer is that I am not among those "wasting opportunities" and "misusing pen and paper" in writing and compiling this tribute to you, my great-Grandfather. I find in you a sort of kindred spirit and feel that I understand your exuberance, convictions, and general outlook on life. I hope that you would not be ashamed of me in bringing up any painful mistakes or memories – God knows you may have been watching over me while I stumbled through every one of my own. Like you, I sought forgiveness and by the grace of God, was able to turn my life around.

In my opinion, you do "possess the faculty of writing amusingly" – and that's a good thing. It makes you human and endearing – and makes you alive in my heart. I am so grateful that you gave me, and the world such wonderful gifts of wisdom and love in the pages of your books.

Donna Wells
January 17, 2017

Chapter One

Meeting the Greiners

"Mr. Gorbachev, tear down this wall!"

Ronald Reagan 1987

"The Berlin Wall and the Iron Curtain were both opened to the general public soon after the announcement by the German Chancellor. It all happened so fast that people where storming the boarder in the middle of the night in anticipation of this. Some border guards stood in disbelief of what just happened. The pick ax and sledge hammer war against the Berlin Wall began within days or even hours of this event.

Claudia and I were following the whole thing on German television. We almost jumped in the car in the middle of the night to drive to Berlin, which thousands of West Germans actually did - armed with whatever it took to "bring down this wall".

Our first journey to what used to be the east was in 1990 or 91 when I contacted Albrecht Greiner-Mai using his contact information he left behind with his artwork in the Weimer Glass Museum."

Jeffrey H. Wells
Great-grandson of Tuisco Greiner

My brother, Jeff, had an important hand in discovering the seeds and deeper roots in Tuisco's family. Like most teenagers, he didn't have much interest in family history, and just wanted to get on with his life. We had at least one thing in common – we both had a rebellious streak in us, and quit school when we had had enough of the high school games and not quite fitting in. So, together we found our way to the nearest Army Recruiting Center. By that time, I was 19, Jeff 17. Somehow, he had convinced Mom and Dad to sign a document giving him permission to join up. The Army took *him*, but they turned me down.

Jeff was young enough and naïve enough to put a condition on his Patriotic Duty. He promised the Army he would join, but only if the Army promised *not* to ship him overseas. HA! Of course, his recruiter was glad to make that promise! And of course, after Basic Training and 18 months at Ft. Hood, TX, he was loaded on a plane heading for the American Army Base in the ancient city of Mainz, Germany. As it turned out, that was just where he needed to be!

Many young American soldiers stationed far from home, fall in love with the native girls. My Uncle, Bud Merrill, was one of them. He served at a U.S Army base office in France, where a tall, beautiful, dark-haired French civilian girl, just happened to work. A letter to my mother tells the story of a secretary named "Monique Marcel Francette Monnot", who sat next to Bud, and flirted with him "all day." Of course, he brought her home and married her! My brother followed suit - except this time, it happened in Germany. He married a girl from Mainz, one of the many young women barely out of high school, that fluttered like moths around a local café where the young, handsome and lonely American soldiers were known to frequent. Claudia Göbig fell in love, despite stern warnings from her family that American Soldiers were notorious for their "love 'em and leave 'em" reputation. Eventually, her parents fell in love with Jeff, too, and so the couple was off on a brief trip to Amsterdam, where they married and spent their honeymoon.

Because Claudia was the youngest in her family, her aging parents counted on her to stay near-by. So, instead of joining her new husband in *his* homeland, he spent the next 35 years living in *hers*... overseas.

By the time Jeff left the Army - after his second tour of duty and two daughters later, he could speak the language enough to get a job on the production line at "Schott's Glas". Four years later, after a back injury, he was transferred to the Security Department, and about a year after that, when the Receptionist at Schott's headquarters suffered a heart attack, Jeff was asked to take his place.

This chain of sometimes unfortunate events, turned out to be very fortunate after all. While in that position, Jeff would meet many high-ranking Schott's people and visitors from around the world. Many of them were intrigued when they learned that he was an American, and were curious to know how he ended up in Germany. The story became more interesting when he related what little he knew of his own family background in glassmaking. What a coincidence to find an American working in Germany for a glassmaking family, whose ancestors had ancient business ties to his own glassmaking ancestors!

His unusual story made a very interesting subject for the company newsletter and (along with a good dose of encouragement from Grandma) sparked a hunger in my brother to learn more about our Greiner ancestors.

And so, a plan was hatched to visit Greiner homelands in Scheibe-Alsbach, Limbach and Lauscha, in the Thuringian forest where our 8th great-Grandfather, Hans "Schwabenhans" Greiner settled in 1585. There, Hans had found the large deposits of sand and limestone, and enough forest to stoke the ovens for years to come – all that was needed to continue the Greiner tradition of glassmaking.

Hans would set up the first *glashutten* (glassworks) there and by 1597 he, along with Christoph Müeller would become co-founders of the town of Lauscha, which would later become the birthplace of the glass eye invented by Ludwig Muller-Uri in 1835, and the home of the first glass Christmas tree ornament – garlands of glass beads, reportedly made by the "Schwabenhans" himself.

Jeff's wife, Claudia was all in to help him in his search. There was only one thing standing in their way… The Berlin Wall. Our ancestors had settled in what would become Russian occupied East Germany, behind "The Iron Curtain".

Eventually, President Reagan declared his famous and most welcomed quote, "Mr. Gorbachev, tear down this wall!" And so, by 1990, they were ready for their first trip. There was nothing to keep Jeff and Claudia from visiting the Greiner homelands by way of beautiful winding, tree lined roads through hills and forests and quaint little villages of red tile roofs – places they would visit again, and again.

The dust from the fallen wall was barely settled, by the time they armed themselves with information from Grandma, and hit the autobahn running - crossing the border into formerly *verboten* territory.

In many ways, it was like stepping into a time warp. Things had not changed much over the years since the "wall" had been in place. Many houses and churches were still sided and roofed with the native gray slate shingles including many homes, churches and business in the area of Scheibe-Alsbach, Thuringia. That's where the slate covered birth home of Tuisco's great-grandfather, Johann Gotthelf Greiner, is located. Gotthelf was born into a long line of glassmakers and is known in that area as "the father of Thuringian porcelain", (a type of Chinese porcelain that had independently and almost simultaneously been "re-invented" by two others.)

DDR Border Eisfeld, Germany 1990

Lauscha Overlook, Thuringen Mountains 1990

Claudia (Göbig) Wells

Photos Courtesy of Jeffrey H. Wells

When Jeff and Claudia told the locals about their reason for being there, they were warmly welcomed, but disappointed to hear how expensive Greiner porcelain had become. Many East German inhabitants had been anxious to earn money for a move to the other side of the broken wall - a more modern world. They sold what valuables they still had at low prices - including Greiner porcelain. They were told, "too bad you didn't come sooner."

Jeff and Claudia would not feel disappointed for long. They would find many Greiner "treasures" in the museums, Greiner homes and former factories. But the best treasure was found in the person of a distant cousin, Rudi Greiner-Adam. They could only take pictures of the museum treasures, and Greiner buildings - they even picked up porcelain figures found in the dirt (most of them broken when Greiner factories were bombed during WWII). But, cousin Rudi would become a family treasure in his own right. He became my brother's family history mentor - almost like a father to him.

Rudi had researched and written much information about the Greiners, which Jeff helped translate into English, including a personal memoir written by our 4th great grandfather, Johann Gotthelf Greiner.

Rudi even spent several years managing, the same porcelain factory in Kloster-Veilsdorf, that Tuisco's grandfather, Ernst Friederich Ferdinand Greiner had managed from 1814, until his death in 1821. Ferdinand's son, Karl Justus Greiner stayed in the business for a time, painting porcelain, and Tuisco followed in the family tradition with his love for inventing and creating beautiful things from... well, if not sand, then dirt.

Tuisco's Great-Grandfather
Johann Gotthelf Greiner
1732-1797

Photo courtesy of Jeffery H. Wells

This is the only known likeness of Johann Gotthelf Greiner to exist. It is thought to have been painted by one of his workers, circa 1800. The cup is located in the Otto Ludwig Museum in Eisfeld, Germany.

Tuisco's grandfather
Ernst Friederich Ferdinand Greiner
1768 - 1821

Photograph of the original portrait taken by Jeffery H. Wells

"The Five Sons of Gotthelf Greiner"
by Ölgemälda von Gottwald Kühn, 1820
Located in the Otto Ludwig Museum in Eisfeld, Germany

L-R Daniel, Friedemann, Florentin, Ernst
Friedrich Ferdinad, Michael Gotthelf

Chapter Two

The Immigrant's Parents

"Our parents had two different characters. Father was idealistic and learned art and science. Mother was real, took care of us and daily household chores."

—August Ludwig "Luie" Greiner
(The immigrant's brother)

Photo Courtesy Dave Olney
"Karl Greiner"

"About our good parents. Father started work at 14 years old because his father died. He learned at his step-brother-laws, Auguste Reinhardt in ____ how to paint porcelain. Besides his job, he went to the academy in Hanan in 1826, Munich 1829, then he was for some time _____ for his brother-in-law, Louis Greiner in Kloster-Veilsdorf, where he left May 24, 1831 with good references. At the time they issued him a passport for one year in Weld-gurghausen.

On the 8th of June, 1831 he got his visa to go from Hamburg to Bernberg. His Christening papers were signed by J. Hoffman, March 31, 1834. His godfathers were Professor Herzog from Bernberg, writer Hennig in Corwig, the wife of Lieutenant Greiner in Gluckstal. When I went to school there, his housekeeper Miss Mathilda Pickel gave me a dinner roll sometimes. He rented an apartment from Ernst Friedrich Naeter. He married Mr. Naeter's daughter Caroline, which was our mother.

Uncle Christel whom we called our second father because of all the good things he did for us, was very proud of her and me. It was very hard for our parents to earn a living. Father helped out his step mother and brother and sisters and nobody could blame our mother for being upset sometimes. But the blessings in the letter from my step grandmother were fulfilled. They were lovingly cared for until their last hour and their blessings, their _____ will carry its fruit.

Our Father often had headaches, but they went away in later years. Probably because he gave up hand painting porcelain."

—August Ludwig "Luie" Greiner

TUISCO GREINER

"In the year . . . father learned from his friend, painter Heinrich Weber in Halle, everything about photography. It was the time it changed from . . . to glass pictures. I helped him out when I was in the service (1855-1857), and stayed with him after. Uncle Christel gave me a small camera with whom I worked for several weeks.

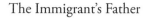

The Immigrant's Father

Karl Justus Greiner
1806-1895

Our parents had two different characters. Father was idealistic and learned art and science. Mother was real, took care of us and daily household chores. We must have inherited traits of both of them and also the good and honorable sentiment. We also hope for a reunion like a short verse our father wrote.

> What is separated in this life
> Will be reunited in young years
> Where the blessed are in heaven
> And are happy at the reunion"
> —Ludwig "Luie" Greiner

"Well do I remember a saying of my good old mother. Whenever she found me, then a young lad, and I fear an often heedless, lad, in company which she did not consider the very best, she used to sound this note of warning; 'Show me with whom you associate, and I will tell you who you are.'

The Immigrant's Mother

Caroline Naeter Greiner
1812-1892

And on certain occasions, banteringly and by way of parodying her well-meant words, I would tell her:
'Show me what you eat, and I will tell you what you are.'
In light of riper experience, I now believe that I was as near right as she was, and that we were both not far out of the way."

Tuisco Greiner
The Garden Book for Practical Farmers 1901 - Pg. 20

Chapter Three

The Immigrants

"I care not what country was the land of my forefathers. This Union of States with its vast opportunities, the productiveness of its farms and gardens, and the wonderful generosity of its climate, is the land of my choice-the grandest country on earth."

Tuisco Greiner
The Garden Book for Practical Farmers (1901)

S.S. Hansa 1861-1883

Karl Gotthold was the first of the three young and unmarried brothers to immigrate to Garlinghouse, Naples, New York. The fourth brother had plans to come later, but had to make the difficult decision to stay behind in Germany. His name was August Ludwig Greiner. They called him Luie. He wrote a family history that was passed down to his niece—my grandmother, Helma Greiner Merrill. How grateful we can be that he included a brief biography of his American bound brothers!

Gotthold

"Brother Gotthold apprenticed as ____ at salesman Roithardt in Nordhausen. He found his job through Hilmar Greiner after he learned how to be a farmer from nephew Oelmann in Nato and went with Nephew Wilhelm Oelhmann to Naples, N. Y. in North America in the year ____. Used his music talents and had a music corps of farmers. He was here for a visit in the year ___ and took music lessons at Lilez and took many instruments back."

The 1855 NYS census record for Naples, notes that William Oehlman, aged 28, arrived in New York about 1848, at the age of 21, and that he had been in town for seven years. The ship "Josephine" left Bremen, Germany and arrived in New York on 17 April 1847 with 20-year-old "Wilh. Ohlman" from Germany. Gotthold (who would have been about 5 years old) was not with him. He was, however, on the ship "Bremen", arriving at the Port of New York, 25 June 1862. With him, was 8-year-old, Fritz Oehlmann, who must have been the nephew.

Gotthold's naturalization papers are dated 24 Sept. 1868, and stated that he had been in the U.S. for 5 years, but only 1 year in New York. A Tax Assessment list from New York City, for Aug.-Sept. 1862 shows that a G. C. Greiner had sold forty-four tables. Gotthold was well-known in Naples, as G.C. Greiner– and as a fine carpenter.

A year later, Gotthold aged 21, had made his way to Naples, and was listed on the "U.S. Civil War Draft Registration Record." I was unable to find any record of him actually serving in the war, although it would have explained his whereabouts for four years, if not in New York.

Seven years later, Tuisco's oldest immigrant brother was settled on his own farm in Garlinghouse, with his wife Jane Bartholomew Greiner and 2 year old daughter, Caroline.

Tuisco

"Brother Tuisco went to a seminar but had to leave because of his free thinking religious direction which didn't harmonize with one of the managers. Then he worked for the Post Office but couldn't keep the job because he couldn't keep things to himself. In the year ___ he went to America, too, went into an institution, but got into a lot of trouble. His sister Helma and brother Otto helped him out a lot and ever since he became a writer about gardening. He seems to be getting better. What a blessing! He lost his dear wife and got married again."

We will learn more about Tuisco's "trouble" in a later chapter…

Tuisco's daughter Helma, wrote about her father, "He must have come to the United States about 1864, as I remember someone said he was about eighteen years old". Tuisco's Naturalization record, of April 1, 1874 has no mention of when he arrived, or how long he had been in the U.S. I believe Helma may have confused Tuisco's arrival, with Friedemann's, since he was eighteen when he immigrated in 1872.

The "U.S. and Canada Passenger and Immigration List" shows a record for 1869 for the S.S. Hansa with a Tuisco, aged 23 and "Gotthaco" Greiner, aged 27. The ages for these two match exactly our immigrant brothers - and since they are also on the same ship that Friedemann arrived on, in 1872, we can *reasonably* assume that these are the Greiner brothers of Naples. Assuming this is true, this would have been Gotthold's second arrival in New York, after returning to Germany to buy musical instruments.

(Note: The above record was transcribed on ancestry.com as "Tensco" and "Gotthaco", although magnification clearly shows "Tuisco" and what looks like "Gotthass." It also shows Tuisco as female. I believe both to be clerical mistakes, since the age and time frame are consistent with that of the brothers'.)

The 1870 U.S. Census record for Naples has no entry for Tuisco, while his brother Gotthold's entry shows that he had literally married "the girl next door", and had a 2-year-old child. Tuisco does not seem to be anywhere in 1870 - but he must have been in Naples in order to have a 3-year-old child with a home grown Garlinghouse girl by 1875. After all, it takes time for a girl to get to know a man, get married, carry a baby for 9 months and then add another 3 years on to that. Again, we can *probably* assume that he was there, but somehow was missed by the census taker.

Friedemann

"Brother Friedmann went to college up to ___ grade___, helped me taking pictures sometimes. Apprenticed in the year ____ at locksmith Rosenthal, who said to his apprentice not too long ago, "You'll never learn in your whole life how to make a lock as good as Mr. Greiner's brother made it after 3 months". He went to America in the year ___. He had a farm and was a bee breeder. All three of them have very good jobs, but it was hard for them to get those jobs. Our good Uncle Christel made it a little easier for them."

Friedemann was the last of the brothers to arrive in Naples. New York. Passenger Lists show a "Friedm Greiner" on the ship "S.S. Hansa", in the "first cabin, lower Saloon", Aged 18, Occupation: Locksmith, Arrival Date: 4 Mar 1872, Port of Departure: Bremen, Germany, Port of Arrival: New York, New York."

No doubts about this Greiner brother's identity! If only all of our ancestor's records were so complete! This record seems to foreshadow a lifelong pattern of perfectionism for Friedemann, that will be seen, as we unfold his story. It's a trait that surfaces again and again, through many of the descendants of the "Schwabenhans" and of Gotthelf Greiner. We can discern this trait in all three of the immigrant brothers, but most prominently in the youngest.

Helma Greiner writes in her life story, "Down Memory Lane", that her father purchased the house in Hunts Hollow in 1874. The

1874 Landownership map for Naples confirms that he did own the farm at that time, It appears from the following newspaper account that Gotthold was making plans to move there, as well.

March 13, 1875, *Naples Record*

"G.C. Greiner has let his farm and will sell all his stock of horses, cows, colts, hay and farming tools. The sale will be positive and with the usual terms. Sale to be on Wednesday, March 17, at 10am. Wm. Marks auctioneer and H. Moulton, auctioneer."

April 3rd, 1875, *Naples Record*

"G.C. Greiner has moved to Hunts Hollow, and James Houghtalin has moved to Greiner's farm."

As of June 1, 1875, The NYS Census record shows the three brothers and their families living together in the same house in Hunts Hollow. Tuisco was 29, and head of household. He is with his wife Hester Bartholomew and they now have a 3-year old daughter, Mary. Gotthold (Charles G.) was 33 and listed as a carpenter. He is married to Hester's sister Jane. They now have two children, Carrie and Charlie. Friedemann was 21 and still single. He and 13-year old Lillian Briggs are listed as servants.

(I wonder if Friedemann knew about that... Oh well, he had the last laugh – he got the house and farm!)

The large stately home is still there overlooking the beautiful ponds that now flank both sides of the Honeoye road above Naples.

A Fourth Immigrant

One more Greiner immigrant made it to Naples after Friedemann arrived - with the plan that the rest of his family would come at a later time.

Brother Luie's son Paul arrived in Garlinghouse October of 1887, and tragically died the following March 1888 – only five months after arriving. His obituary gives an emotional and poignant account:

Naples Record March 7, 1888 Garlinghouse

"...It is seldom, if ever, a heavier blow has fallen upon this community. All both old and young, lament his most untimely death and mourn and sympathize with his brothers and sisters at home, and we hope and pray God's grace may sustain and comfort them in this the saddest bereavement of their lives. A very large concourse of people attended his funeral on Saturday, March 10, 1888, the Rev. J.H. Masten officiating. He quietly sleeps in our cemetery here..."

Brother Luie's description of his brothers ended with this comment:
"God bless them. If Paul hadn't been killed in an accident, we would be with them now."

Paul's death would be one of the first of many heartbreaking tragedies for the three Greiner brothers of Naples, NY. These accounts, as well as Paul's complete obituary can be found in chapter ten of this book, "Heartbreak and Tragedy."

Chapter Four

Golden Years of Garlinghouse

"John Garlinghouse... afterwards settled in what is now called the "Garlinghouse Settlement."

Orson Walbridge 1887

Early History of the Town of Springwater, Livingston County

Garlinghouse District 8 Schoolhouse

"The house was completed and first used for Sunday School and prayer services January 19, 1888, S. J. Merrill then having the

Sunday School in charge. The first sermon in the house was preached by Rev. J.H. Masten on February 19, 1888."

S.J. Merrill
Naples Record, January 20, 1915

The schoolhouse pictured, is now used as a private home. According to the same article, the original schoolhouse was a log building that was moved there in 1843 from my 2nd Great-Grandfather, David Briggs' farm. It was replaced in 1852, with a frame building, that the founders named "Little Zion". That would have been where the Greiner Brother's attended church. David Briggs' Great-Grandson, and my grandfather, Raymond Briggs Merrill, taught school in the 1888 schoolhouse starting in 1914. Supposedly all the girls had a crush on him, but his student, Tuisco Greiner's daughter Helma, proved to be the most persistent. She flirted with a boy, which drove Ray into a jealous anger, prompting him to action. They married June, 1923. He was almost 30, she was 18.

(The Authot of this book)

Not long after arriving in Garlinghouse, Tuisco married Hester Bartholomew. Her sister Jane had already married Tuisco's brother Gotthold. The Bartholomew girls were born and raised in the secluded little hamlet of Garlinghouse, back when the level tops of the hills were cleared of forest, making way for cultivated fields, and where the Greiner brothers had first settled.

Tuisco and Hester had four children. Mary was born in Garlinghouse in 1872, Zora in 1875, and Louis, 1879. Both Zora and Mary were born in Hunts Hollow. Otto would arrive in 1887 while they were living in Little Silver, NJ.

I don't know why the Greiner brother's relative, William Oehlman first chose to settle in Garlinghouse. It surely is a beautiful place - a snug little community in a hollow that traces a narrow, winding path through the hills outside of Naples. My mother's side of the family all settled there, starting in the 1840's. They spent many years marrying their neighbors and cousins and raising their families there.

From the time I was barely old enough to remember, we would often drive Grandma through Garlinghouse, to satisfy her longing to remember, and to be among the family she missed so much. We would go in the spring, when the white Trillium were in bloom in the forest - for no other reason than to look at what few houses were left, read familiar names on the stones in the cemetery, and listen to Grandma's stories of the families that had lived there and were interred there. Even though I didn't remember much of what she said, the seed she planted, would eventually grow in my mind and heart.

On the uppermost hill, we often walked a dirt path along the edge of a dense forest of deciduous and evergreen trees to an awe-inspiring view - one that I can imagine my ancestors and even the Seneca before them, paused to admire. Just before the hillside starts to plunge downward, we catch sight of the gleaming, silver sliver of Honeoye Lake shimmering in the distance, nestled along the bottom of the lush green Honeoye Valley, looking, from that distance, more like a puddle leftover from the glacial retreat.

The Hunts Hollow Road and the houses below are hidden among the trees. Anyone taking the time to pause there, cannot help but notice a sweet, restful peace settling deep in the soul. I imagined that the view and the feeling was no different than when the native Seneca lived there.

If we could walk down the steep side of the hill, we would be in Hunts Hollow, where the Greiner immigrant brothers would soon move.

A very brief description of the origins of the present hamlet of Garlinghouse and Hunts Hollow is found in the book, "Early History of the Town of Springwater, Livingston County" by Orson

Walbridge 1887. The article included in the book was written by D. B. Waite, Hunts Hollow.

"The First Settlement in the Town of Springwater"

"James and John Garlinghouse the next year put up a cabin on the line a little west of the present saw mill, and became the first actual resident of the town, and here Mary Garlinghouse was born in June, 1797, and was the first white child born in town. She became in time the wife of Thomas Briggs, of whom we shall speak hereafter. James Garlinghouse married Elanor Hunt, a sister to Aaron. T."

"John Garlinghouse and his Nephew, Benjamin, afterwards settled in what is now called the "Garlinghouse Settlement." John afterwards went to Richmond, died there …."

A little hamlet, in the town of Richmond, north of Honeoye, called Allen's Hill, claims the resting place of this John Garlinghouse. It's ironic that Garlinghouse and Allens Hill both have just a sliver's view of Honeoye Lake. I wonder if John realized that, when he moved up the Honeoye valley.

There, he would be closer to the Ontario County seat, of Canandaigua, or "Ga-nun-da-gwa", as the Seneca called it, translated as "The Chosen Spot." John's Great-Granddaughter, Caroline was born there in 1856. She would become the great-grandmother of Katherine Hepburn. Later, in her autobiography, Katherine would mention spending summers with her Houghton relatives there. Canandaigua Lake was, and is, a popular summer resort that stretches 16 miles from Canandaigua to Naples.

Many years ago, Stuart (Casey) Case, an elderly neighbor, in Naples, shared with me a story from his childhood. He was hired as a summer play mate for another well-known child celebrity-to-be, summer resident of Canandaigua area, Humphrey Bogart.

Casey was not the type to tell tall tales, even so, I had a hard time believing his story. Eventually, I researched his claim, and was surprised to find in the 1900 census, Belmont D. Bogart, Maude Bogart and their 5-month-old son, Humphrey D. Bogart, living in South Bristol, between Naples and Canandaigua. With them, was a servant, a nurse, and a laborer.

I can't help but wonder if Humphrey ever shared with his fellow actor, childhood memories of carefree summers on beautiful Canandaigua Lake, with a wiry boy from Naples named Casey. I wonder, too, if Katherine ever visited the little hamlet named after her third great-grandfather, John Garlinghouse.

The Greiner Brothers didn't stay long in Garlinghouse before they moved to Hunts Hollow, but they were still not far away, and so continued to be a part of the social scene there. Here, we get an idea of the early impact Tuisco had on the community:

August 14, 1875 – *Naples Record*

"On Friday evening of last week the Scholars and teachers of the Garlinghouse Sabbath School with ample provisions for the occasion and a copy of Dr. Livingstone's Travels sold by Hancock, made Tuisco Greiner a call. Tuisco had taught the school music and was much respected by all.

They arrived late at the Greiner's house on the Ben French farm, and was completely surprised by the filing in of his pupils and associates. They played and sang some good Sunday School songs, and then S.J. Merrill stepped out with a copy of Livingstone's Travels in his hands and in a neat speech presented it to Mr. Greiner in behalf of the Garlinghouse School. Mr. Greiner was too much surprised to speak much, but evinced his gratitude in every other way. The tables were ____ and enjoyment was the order ____ more singing and a happy ____ the school returned home."

I regret that I was not as grateful a student, when Tuisco's daughter Helma, attempted to teach her stubborn granddaughter how to play the piano!

The brothers separated again, when Gotthold moved back to Garlinghouse sometime after 1880. He is found there in the 1892 NYS census record which shows Gotthold in the Town of Naples, surrounded by known Garlinghouse residents. By 1900 both he and brother Tuisco would be reunited in La Salle, Niagara, NY and Friedemann would spend the rest of his days in the beautiful Hunts Hollow home, in Naples.

Gradually, as the Garlinghouse families grew older, many of them moved to North Cohocton-Atlanta, to a more convenient village location. Some had already been renting homes in the village of Naples during the winter to avoid the steep and snowy roads of Garlinghouse. The Greiner brothers relative, William Oehlman was one of them. The 1875 Land ownership map of the village of Naples shows "William Oehlman's Spring residence", on Main St. in the village, along with a large vineyard on the opposite side of the street. Those were more prosperous times in the growing little village.

And so, the population dwindled, and many of the homes of the early settlers of Garlinghouse are now gone, as well.

From 1844, when Tuisco's grandfather-in-law, Aaron Bartholomew first settled in Garlinghouse, to about 1925 when his daughter and son-in-law, Helma and Ray Merrill moved away, a total of about 86 golden years of forming life-long friendships and close family ties in the beautiful little hamlet above Naples, had passed.

Chapter Five

A Booming Business

"It should be a gratifying fact to every citizen in Naples that Mr. Greiner has built up so large a seed business in so short a time, and it is certainly an indication of far greater success in the future."

The Naples Record, March 3, 1881

Courtesy The Naples Library, Photo Archives

Main Street Naples looking south, c.1871
Tuisco's store was located somewhere across
the street from the church steeple.

The 1875 N.Y.S. Census record, shows Gotthold as being a carpenter, while Tuisco was still listed as a farmer. Their occupations would evolve over time, as more and more newspaper ads started appearing in the Naples Record:

January 22, 1876- *Naples Record*

"The Greiner Brothers at the head of Hunts Hollow have made and have on hand two new, well made and finished sleighs; they warrant the wood work and ironing to be of the best; they wish to sell them at reasonable prices. They can be seen at their residence near French's and all who want will be satisfied when they examine them. They give notice that they will make to order and repair anything in the sleigh; line and warrant their work. Call on them."

January 22, 1876- *Naples Record*

"F.H. Frink and G.C. Greiner both of this town have secured the right to manufacture and sell the celebrated Alverson Union Bee Hive and will supply the town the coming season. Greiner Brothers will do all the transferring from any old hive to the above named hive as soon as the season will admit, for all who may call on them."

February 5, 1876- *Naples Record*

"F.H. Frink has sold out his interest in the Union Bee Hive to Greiner Brothers, who will now attend to all who want. G. G. Greiner has been out a couple of days and took orders for fifty hives . . . so . . . is the rush for them. It is a fine . . . and every bee grower needs just as many as he has swarms."

February 24, 1877- *Naples Record*

"Tuisco Greiner has started a branch of industry that commends itself to all of our people. He will put up for spring use the ordinary garden seeds needed; they will be true to name and nature. He raised some varieties and imports from Europe others – he will put into neat packages; just what our people needs – the enterprise is a good one and we trust he will receive the support of this community in building up such an industry."

May 24, 1879- *Naples Record*
(From an article on the history of Hunts Hollow)

"Rochester is not much ahead of us on vegetable and flower seeds, as Tuisco Greiner is a first class gardener, and has his Seed Catalogue and Price List in the hands of many seed dealers and farmers. We can recommend his seeds first-class, as we have tried them and know. As for fruit, we will not take a back seat on any locality in this country; we can raise any kind of fruit, and as much as any vicinity in Western New York."

As the brothers prospered in their business, Friedemann would strike out on his own. He purchased 10 acres of the Hunts Hollow farm that Tuisco had originally purchased in 1874.

January 4, 1879- *Naples Record*,

"The following are recent conveyances of real estate in the town of Naples… Tuisco Greiner, et. un., Freedman Greiner, $1000…."

By the 1880 US census, the family was growing, and probably needing more space. Tuisco and his family are in the same house, while Gotthold, his family, and still single Friedemann are all together in a house next door. Both Gotthold and Friedemann's occupations had changed from farmer and servant to beekeepers. Tuisco is now listed as a "seedsman from Prussia." With him is his wife, Hester, 28, and their children—Mary E., 7; Zora, 4; and Louis, 1.

Newspaper ads abounded in the next few years as Tuisco's business enterprises multiplied in number and grew in scope. Some ads would reveal Tuisco's exuberant personality in amusing ways.

July 22, 1880- *Naples Record*

"Tuisco Greiner will boost out your stumps in a hurry. See his advertisement.

Stumps Removed and Split, and Rocks blasted by the use of Giant Powder, at Small Cost! Contracts taken now. Inquire of TUISCO GREINER."

To the delight of the town of Naples, Tuisco's business ventures ballooned to new heights over the next two years:

A Travel Agent:
February 17, 1882-*Naples Record*

"Passage Tickets to and from Germany. I wish to say to my German friends that I am an agent for the North German Lloyd Line of Bremen, and that I sell tickets for an ocean and railroad passage from all railway stations in Germany to any railway station in the United States, or from here to Bremen; also round trip tickets. Any information on this matter will be cheerfully given. Call and See me. Tuisco Greiner"

A Seed and Grocery Store:

March 3, 1881- *The Neapolitan*

"Tuisco Greiner is preparing C. M. Lyon's store, near the Stewart House, and will open a seed store there in a few days."

March 3, 1882- *Naples Record*

"Mr. Tuisco Greiner now fairly located in Housel's new store, is sending through our post office some 12,000 seed catalogues and is preparing in every way for a large business this season. His store will be, when completely fitted, as neat as any in our town. It should be a gratifying fact to every citizen in Naples that Mr. Greiner has built up so large a seed business in so short a time, and it is certainly an indication of far greater success in the future."

March 24, 1882- *The Neapolitan*

"The seed store of Tuisco Greiner is welcome in our midst. It pleases good citizens to see our towns' industries increase. And we ask for him the hearty support of the entire community. His seeds are of the best and he is a worthy, reliable dealer. Anything in the seed or plant line that he has not on hand he will get for you cheaper than you can. By all means give him a visit for what you want."

January 27, 1882- *Naples Record*

"Tuisco Greiner has purchased the stock of L.L. Sutton, and rented the store for a term of years, Mr. Greiner will now have a fine location for his extensive business as a seedsman and will continue the grocery trade."

February 9, 1882- *The Neapolitan*

"Tuisco Greiner has secured the new store recently built by Henry Housel, opposite The Stewart House and will open the seed business in good season."

May 4, 1882- *The Neapolitan*

"Tuisco Greiner had this week ripe strawberries in his store; they were of the Sharpless, variety, and from his greenhouse."

April 7, 1882- *Naples Record*

"Russian white oats for sale   TUISCO GREINER"

"All sorts of seeds, seed potatoes, grass and clover seed, choice grape vines, etc.; also, sugar cane seed, at TUISCO GREINER's"

June 8, 1882- *The Neapolitan*

"Tuisco Greiner has a fertilizer that not only is in itself, valuable in that way but proves to be death to Currant worms and the different species of bugs that are sure to break the christian Sabbath by their devastations in your gardens; ask him about it at the seed store."

April 20, 1883- *Naples Record*

"Good seeds, good plants, and don't you forget it, at Tuisco Greiner's."

Printing Supplies, Etc.

April 7, 1882- *Naples Record*

"I can furnish rubber stamps, clothing markers, and rubber type on short notice, and very cheap.   TUISCO GREINER"

Magazine Publisher & Event Organizer:

January 26, 1882- *The Neapolitan*

"On Tuesday Jan. 31st, there will be a lecture on sugar-cane growing at the Town Hall by C. J. Reynolds, of Corning, N.Y. This is the one promised by Tuisco Greiner and the farmers should attend. Lecture free at 1:30 p. m. Other speakers are expected, and a general discussion will be enjoyed."

February 16, 1882- *The Neapolitan*

"Tuisco Greiner "Garden Talks" is out. He has twelve thousand for distribution and is a very valuable quarterly."

February 17, 1882- *Naples Record*

"Number one of Garden Talks, an illustrated quarterly magazine and guide, for the home and market garden, has been received. It is a very neat publication, and as its title indicates, full of information about seeds and vegetables, and everything connected with the garden. It is conducted by our townsman, Tuisco Greiner, and deserves, and doubtless will, reach a large circulation. It also contains his annual price list of vegetables and flower seeds. Send ten cents to Mr. Greiner, and receive this and the three succeeding numbers."

October 6, 1882- *Naples Record*

"We take considerable pride in calling attention to the large amount of job work done recently at the RECORD office, a part of which is the third number of Garden Talks, the horticultural quarterly magazine published by Tuisco Greiner, a large edition of which has just been issued…."

January 10, 1883- *Naples Record*

"The fourth number of Garden Talks, the popular horticultural quarterly magazine published by Tuisco Greiner, has just been issued. Its earlier appearance has been unavoidably delayed, but it's unusually interesting contents, and its neat appearance, will in measure make up for the delay. Every gardener and lover of flowers and plants should have a copy. It was printed at the Record Office."

An Oyster Bar:
(an oyster bar?)

October 12, 1882- *The Neapolitan*

"Tuisco Greiner expects to open up his "Oyster Bar" on Saturday evening of this week. He intends to be headquarters in oysters, cigars, etc., at his store opposite The Stewart House. See this advertisement for particulars.

OYSTERS.

This week will be the preparation for a

FIRST-CLASS
OYSTER DEPOT
AT NAPLES.

Come to my place of business opposite the Stewart House and get

FRESH, NICE, OYSTERS

Cooked in any way; and by the MEASURE
The choicest BRANDS OF CIGARS, and CANDIES on hand.
Call In
Tuisco Greiner"

March 2, 1883- *Naples Record*

"Remember, Tuisco Greiner's Oyster Saloon where you can get a full dish of fresh oysters, raw, stewed or fried; also, a splendid assortment of cigars and tobacco, candies, etc."

Well, as the saying goes... what goes up must come down. Three short years after opening his first store, we find a hint of too many eggs in one basket about to drop in a heap of slimy ruin...

March 29, 1883- *The Neapolitan*

"Being so busy with the seed business Tuisco Greiner will close his saloon from this date.

TUISCO GREINER

TUISCO GREINER The Oyster season is over, but I still keep fine SALMON, LOBSTER, SARDINES, ETC., If you are in need of SEEDS, VEGETABLE or FLOWER, SEED POTATOES, GARDEN IMPLEMENTS, PLANTS, ETC., call and see me. I have a very choice lot of ONION and CABBAGE seeds in any quantity required. - Remember my store opposite Luther's Hotel - Tuisco Greiner Publisher of Garden Talk."

April 5, 1883- *Naples Record*
(Three ads this week)

"Special rates for clover seed in large quantities."

Tuisco Greiner

"Tuisco Greiner keeps on hand all kinds of seeds, fresh and genuine. Call on him."

"From now until further notice my Saloon will be closed, as the seed business requires my undivided attention. Tuisco Greiner"

April 5, 1883- *The Neapolitan*

"TUISCO Greiner The Oyster season is over, but I still keep fine SALMON, LOBSTER, SARDINES, ETC., If you are in need of SEEDS, VEGETABLE or FLOWER, SEED POTATOES, GARDEN IMPLEMENTS, PLANTS, ETC., call and see me.
I have a very choice lot of ONION and CABBAGE seeds in any quantity required. Remember my store opposite Luther's Hotel."

Tuisco Greiner Publisher of Garden Talk

"Good seeds, good plants and don't you forget it, at Tuisco Greiner's.
The best fertilizer, because most concentrated, strongest, is the Bowker, sold by Tuisco Greiner.

Tuisco Greiner says, farmers should step in and give their order for the celebrated Bowker's phosphates, the best and most concentrated fertilizer in the market. He will furnish it only on order."

April 20, 1883- *Naples Record*

- Special Rates for clover seed in large quantities. Tuisco Greiner.
- Tuisco Greiner keeps on hand all kinds of seeds, fresh and genuine. Call on him.
- I need room for seeds, and will sell candies and tobaccos at reduced rates. Tuisco Greiner.
- Farmers in need of a good phosphate will please call at Tuisco Greiner's and leave their order for the celebrated Bowker Grain Fertiliser. This is the best because strongest phosphate in the market, and pays well. Don't delay, for he says he can furnish it only when order is given now.

By the time I finished reading all the ads and articles, I was out of breath thinking of Tuisco running himself ragged, with the realization that he was in trouble, and too late to fix it.

What happened only six days later, was unimaginably shocking to Tuisco's customers, friends and family – including me, 133 years after the fact.

Chapter Six

"The Change"

"The only advice I can give in such cases is, keep your hands off all larger operations until you know the outcome of the smaller ones."

Tuisco Greiner
The Garden Book for Practical Farmers – 1901, Pg. 19

Tuisco was 37 years old, and it seemed he was on top of the world, yet only two weeks after the Oyster Saloon closed, the rest of the basket of eggs dropped. During the next few weeks everything Tuisco had worked for was gone. The tide of happy support for Tuisco's endeavors turned quickly against him.

The Naples Record detailed the account from the shocking beginning to the bitterly painful end…

April 26, 1883

"The excitement on "the Change" this morning was great on account of the disappearance of Tuisco Greiner yesterday. His creditors

have been issuing attachments to-day to cover what he had. His wife, children and other relatives are as astonished as any at the unhappy state of affairs, and in no way compromised by any crookedness of his. It is to be regretted in any community. As we close our columns the full facts are not known."

April 27, 1883
Debt, Deviltry, Desertion and Disgrace!

"Yesterday was another lively day in financial circles. There was a skipping to and fro and much talk, but sad to say, but very little wool. It was first generally known early yesterday morning that Tuisco Greiner, our restaurantist, and seedsman, had slipped his halter and retired from the scenes of his late business.

He left town on Wednesday morning, taking the cars at Bloods for the east, leaving his store closed. From recent developments, this excited some suspicion, and a black rag tied to the door latch on Wednesday, indicated some thought. By night, some of his creditors guessed at the state of affairs and proceeded as best they might to realize. But not until yesterday did the full inwardress of its escapade dawn upon the community. Claim after claim came to light, forged paper was produced, many an unsuspecting man found himself victimized. It was sad and sickening, and the more so because of the confidence which until quite lately has been so freely bestowed upon the departed. It now looks as though his indebtedness would foot up between $3500 and $4000 with but little to pay with; and worst of all is the forged papers. We have heard as yet of but three parties whose names were forged – that of A. Bartholomew, his father-in-law, David Bartholomew, his brother-in-law, and F. Greiner, his brother.

Their paper will amount to $700 or $800. There is much speculation as to the immediate cause of the failure. We have our opinions and doubtless others have theirs. The village gladly welcomed Mr. G. here some four years ago and encouraged him to start a seed store, as long as he worked at his legitimate business as he prospered.

When he struck out defiantly in a dangerous path the death knell was sounded. We admired his genius, and have greatly respected him. We have trusted him, as our little deficit of $150 will show; and we most deeply regret outside of all monetary consideration his downfall. For his family, especially, we have a heartfelt sorrow; and for his creditors, well, we know how it is ourselves. It has been attempted to intercept his flight, but he does not propose to be brought back here alive, and we do not expect to see him. Messer's Granby Bro's are the lucky ones, who secure his stock in trade; what will be done with it remains to be seen."

Numerous articles appeared in the May 3, 1883 edition of the Naples Record. It seemed everyone wanted a piece of the action:

May 3, 1883

"Saturday was a lively day on the street; the Greiner affair was the main cause.

Those seeds from Greiners are at Granby's they have no use for them and will almost give them away.

The Granby Bro's have moved the seeds to their store – from Greiner's. They don't want them; so go and get in any quantity.

Some suits are likely to grow out of the Tuisco Greiner matters, but Reed and Pottle can get up suits that will excel all such and be cheaper.

Yesterday, the goods and fixtures at the store of Tuisco Greiner were sold by Granby Bro's upon a chattel mortgage given to H.C. Whitman, just before he left the country, and by him assigned to the Granby's. The sale was well attended.

The Tuisco Greiner affair is the nine-day wonder of the town. Considerable of his paper, claimed by the endorsers to be forged, has come to light. Aaron and David B. Bartholomew are the names used. Of course, they will pay no attention in any case, where their names have been used by him without consent, and the loss will fall upon the holders. There are several of these notes. Attachments were placed on all of his property and it has been sold according to law. The Granby Bro's were the first to act and pushed the matter through as fast as the law would allow; the unfortunate affair has created quite a sensation as Mr. Greiner had the confidence of our community until just recently, and the turn in his affairs was unexpected. The loss to our community in unpaid liabilities aggregates over $5000, and what outside dealers will lose is not known. The respected wife and children have the sympathy of the entire community and the remaining brothers, in the bee and farming business are not at all discredited by any of the transactions of the brother, but stand above reproach in any way. A list of the losses cannot be given entire and it would not be advisable to give it; suffice to say, in some cases, it falls where it cannot be spared without feeling."

May 4, 1883
The Greiner Donation

"The creditors of the Greiner "shrinking fund" to the amount of $100 and upwards read as follows;

Friedemann Greiner	$500
Record Office	$150
Edward A. Jones	$300
David Bartholomew	$100
Horace Gillett	$300
Charles Miner	$100
Granby Bro's	$225
G.A. Gordon	$100
H.C. Whitman	$250
John Legore	$100
H.H. Torrey	$200
F.M. Pottle	$100
Sam Boles	$200

Charles Bailey	....	$100
I.C. Williams	....	$200
Wm. E. Lincoln	....	$100
Edwin Hinkley	....	$180

These amounts add up to $3200, while the number of claims in sums less than $100 is legion, the total indebtedness reaching to about $6000. Some $1700 of this is in forged notes. Of these, that of H.H. Torrey has been provided for, and the real and personal estate of Greiner, which has been seized, will possibly reach $900, H.C. Whitman escapes with a whole hide and several others will lose but little: but most of the creditors will lose all."

May 4, 1883

"The Sherriff's sale of the Greiner stock of seeds, etc. in part took place Wednesday, and was quite lively. H.A. Housel made a first class auctioneer. The property owned by the Granby Mortgage will nearly clean out their claim. The sale was adjourned till next Tuesday.

Granby Bro's purchased the stock of seeds owned by Greiner, and don't want them; and will ___ prices on seed in large or small quantities that cannot help but please, as they are all to be closed out.

Suit has been entered by Samuel Boles against Aaron Bartholomew, to recover on the Greiner note held by Boles, which has upon it the forged signature of the defendant."

May 8, 1883

"Jordan Bros., for their debt against Tuisco Greiner, seized upon some choice potatoes at Bloods Depot which were billed to Greiner, and closed them out so successfully as to indemnify then in full. They sold four barrels for $16 per barrel to Eber Weld, of Prattsburgh. They were of a variety known as "Walls Orange," and said to be very superior."

May 16, 1883- *Watkins Democrat,* Watkins, NY

"—The absconded Tuisco Greiner, of Naples, proves to be a villain of larger magnitude than was at first supposed. His total indebtedness is about $5,500, for part of which he had issued forged notes amounting to $1,700. His dishonest operations began about a year ago. An effort will be made to collect some of the forged obligations, on the ground that the relative whose name was used had in a measure acknowledged the claim, though denying the signature."

Six months later, Tuisco was found in a "bad way":

Oct 26, 1883- Richmond, Va.

"– A man giving the name of Joseph Harding was arrested here last evening by Detective John Wren on a charge of forgery committed in Naples, Ontario county, N.Y. The man had been followed for several days by the detective, awaiting the arrival of F. G. Cramer, one of the parties of whose name had been forged. Mr. Cramer identified the prisoner as the criminal, and stated that his real name is Tuisco Greiner. His forgeries on different parties amount to several thousand dollars."

November 7, 1883-*The Penn Yan Express*
Tuisco Greiner

"A paragraph in the Rochester Democrat and Chronicle of Tuesday last, stated that Tuisco Greiner, alias Joseph Harding had been arrested in Richmond, V.A., for forgery. It has since developed that the arrest was made at the instance of F.G. Cramer of this village, who went personally as one of the creditors of Mr. Greiner, to secure his debt. The matter of discovery and arrest was very well worked up, and we believe that the result has warranted the effort. Mr. Greiner was living in a state of comparative privation and distress. He was earning a small amount by writing for an agricultural publication, and was about perfecting a contrivance for forcing the fattening of fowls. He confesses to a miserably unhappy life since he left this town. Mr. Cramer returned on Monday, but was not accompanied by the prisoner and his whereabouts at present we have no way of knowing. -Naples Record"

November 7, 1883 - *Hammondsport, N.Y. Herald*

"—Tuisco Greiner, who lately forged a paper to the amount of several thousand dollars at Naples, has been found by detectives living at Richmond, Va., under the assumed name of Joseph Harding."

Nov. 8, 1883- *Prattsbugh News*

"Some months ago Tuisco Greiner of Naples suddenly decamped between two days, leaving numerous creditors to mourn his departure. By reference to the following Associate Press dispatch, recently published in the New York Tribune, it will be seen that Mr. Greiner has been arrested in Richmond, Va., at the instance of Frank G. Cramer, and will undoubtedly be constrained to return to his home."

November 14, 1883- *The Steuben Advocate* Bath, N.Y.

"—Tuisco Greiner was arrested at Richmond, Va., on account of forgery committed on some Naples merchants."

Finally, a letter of explanation from the "absconded" – along with a little defense, a little pathos, a little drama, and a lot of regret. No one could ever accuse Tuisco Greiner of being boring...

An Open Letter

"Regretting deeply the disappointment caused by me to my townspeople, I wish to say, that never in my life has it been my purpose to defraud anyone of a single cent; and that it is the foremost aim of my life to obtain, by honest labor the means of paying back every cent I owe, thus redeeming my name as far as possible.

It will be hardly necessary to vindicate my general character. The best people of town know that nine-tenths of the floating reports about me are absurd, and originate in idle gossip. My sins have been sins of the head, not of the heart; sins of miscalculations but not of intent.

Some one (sic) had charged me with dissipation! Who has ever seen me drunk, or use any kind of strong drink as a beverage? Speak out now, or forever hold your peace! Who can say up to the time I left Naples, with less than $3 in my pocket, I have not tried to deal fair and, square, and honestly with him?

Who has observed anything mean or low, or contemptible in my behavior? I, who should know best, say I have not. I have in some cases been carried too far, much too far, by misplaced sympathies, and thus been open to severe and perhaps not undeserved criticisms; I have been unwise and imprudent, but low, mean or dishonest, never!

And the penalty of my imprudence? The work of 8 or more years has come to naught! What I had intended should become a proud structure to stand firm for years to come, has tumbled into ruins, and my good name with it, the name for which I had aimed to earn a national reputation. I have lost home and family, perhaps for years, and must be a stranger among strangers, wandering from place to place and be hunted down in reality or imagination, like a wild beast!

Made for a quiet home life, I am lost in the wilderness. In unbounded love for my wife and children and yearning to go to them, I am compelled to turn my back on them! But why do I lay open before the world -cold, selfish and unsympathetic world- all my troubles, only to be sneered at, criticized and ridiculed?

Treasures are left, of which no one can deprive me – the unselfish, self-sacrificing love of brothers, the unwavering and increasing love of a beloved wife, the implicit faith and devotion of three loving children, and considerable self respect and hope for the better. Yours etc. TUISCO GREINER, The Neapolitan – November 22, 1883"

One anonymous writer was not very impressed:

November 29, 1883- *Ontario Messenger*, Canandaigua, N. Y.

"The Neapolitan prints a half-column "open letter" from the absconded Tuisco Greiner, late of Naples, dated from nowhere, "November, 1883," in which he claims to have been unfortunate in business, instead of criminal, and bewails the fact that he is separated from his home and dear ones there. We presume that his 'little' obligation to Mr. G. Frank Cramer has been settled by relatives, or else he would be brought here from Virginia, to answer a serious charge against him."

Thankfully, the wounds would eventually heal, and family would pitch in to help pay at least some of the debt. Friedemann would be the highest bidder for the house and farm at the Sherriff's sale, thereby keeping it in the Greiner family for many years to come.

February 20, 1884- *The Steuben Advocate*, Bath, N.Y.

"—Tuisco Greiner's brothers have taken up his forged paper in Naples, paying fifty cents on the dollar"

6 August 1884- Sherriff's Sale
Supreme Court – County of Ontario, ss –

Friedemann Greiner vs. Tuisco Greiner.

"By virtue of one Execution issued out of the Supreme Court of the State of New York, to me directed and delivered, against the goods and chattel, lands and tenements of Tuisco Greiner, I have seized and taken all the rights, titles and interest of said defendant, in and to the described property to wit: All the interest of the in about twenty acres of land being one-half the interest therein: said land described as follows:

"All that tract or parcel of land situate in the town of Naples aforesaid, being a part of lots number seven and in the eleventh Range of lots.

Which property I shall offer for sale, as the law directs, on the 20th day of September 1884, at one o'clock in the afternoon, at the House on the above described premises in the town of Naples, County of Ontario, N.Y.

Dated this 6th day of August 1884. Hiram Peck, Sherriff By Chas. L. Granby Deputy Sherriff"

I was so stunned by these revelations, I wanted to cry. I know what it's like to make mistakes big enough to hurt family and friends. I know what it's like to be haunted by shame and regret, and not know what to do about it, except to hide. I can imagine Tuisco in a small, dark hovel with little to eat and no friends left to speak of. As someone once told me, "You play, you pay." And I did, and he would – for a very long time…

The good news is, that over time, Naples would forgive and heal, and Tuisco would make amends.

April 23, 1890-*Naples Record*

"All who have just claims against me will please hand a statement of nature, date and original amount of such claim to my brother, G.C. Greiner, Naples, N.Y. or forward same to my address at an early date. Tuisco Greiner, La Salle, N.Y."

Chapter Seven

A Time to Forgive

"He is a valuable adjunct to any paper of that stripe."

Naples Record, 1885

Courtesy thegraphicsfairy.com

    Undoubtedly Tuisco was a humbled and repentant man. The whole experience must have taught him a valuable lesson in sound business practices, however, his wonderful exuberant spirit survived, as we will see later.

By 1885 Tuisco and his family had moved to Little Silver, New Jersey where he would continue writing about his agricultural experiments - a less meteoric career, but with all the energy and exuberance he had put into his former activities.

November 25, 1885- *Red Bank Register*, Red Bank, NJ
Personal Column

"Tuisco Greiner and family are now occupying the old homestead on the Farrier Place at Little Silver, where he has made a number of improvements. Mr. Greiner is a native of Germany, and is the author of several works on horticulture. He has been engaged as editor of John T. Lovett's new horticultural paper, Orchard and Garden."

It seems that the Naples community responded favorably. It's clear that, at least some, had forgiven their wayward townsman for the debacle that shocked them only two years before. At least one newspaper writer in Naples was regaining a measure of respect, for the man he briefly considered an arch enemy:

August 19, 1885- *Naples Record*

"Tuisco Greiner has accepted a position on the "Orchard and Garden" a paper of New Jersey. He is a valuable adjunct to any paper of that stripe."

October 1885- *Canandaigua, N.Y., Repository and Messenger*

"Tuisco Greiner, late of Naples, is publishing a horticultural monthly at Little Silver, N. J., entitled "The Orchard and Garden."

February 16, 1887- *Naples Record*

"The 'Orchard and Garden' is a first class monthly, published by J. T. Lovett at Little Silver, NJ. It is only 50 cents and worth several times that to fruit growers. Tuisco Greiner is connected with the Journal which is an evidence of it's worth."

Tuisco was also a member of the American Horticultural Society and was a speaker at their conventions:

"Transactions of the American Horticultural Society, Volume 4. For the Year 1886"

"Standing Committees… On the Rural Press… Tuisco Greiner of New Jersey." - Pg 9

"Members… Tuisco Greiner, Editor Orchard and Garden, Little Silver, New Jersey." - Pg 16

"A very creditable delegation, consisting of leading horticulturists and press representatives from a large number of the States, was present at the opening session. Among the press representatives were the following: Tuisco Greiner, Orchard and Garden, Little Silver, N.J." - Pg 25

"On resuming the chair at 2 p.m. President Earle introduced the afternoon session by presenting Mr. Greiner of New Jersey, who read his paper on Transplanting." - Pg. 82

The article was printed in full – a little dry unless you are an avid gardener. It was worth reading, just to get an appreciation of Tuisco's personality through the occasional delightful analogies:

"Transplanting in Theory and Practice By Tusico Greiner of New Jersey."

….."How can you invariably succeed in making plants live and thrive? *First catch your plants.* Do not catch them in a patch of weeds where they are trying to hide their deficiencies. Do not catch them in a crowd; long legged, weak kneed, dudish looking things, without bone or marrow, composed mainly of water and gas, and ready to wilt down before the first ray of sunlight. Catch stout, stocky, hearty, well developed plants..."

(Advice that could just as well be considered by a woman in search of a good man.)

And Tuisco would be on hand as a translator:

Convention Minutes.

"Full Text of the Experiment Station Bill as enacted by Congress and Approved by the President March 3, 1887.... Third Day—Thursday. Afternoon Session. At 2 o'clock the Society was again called to order.
President Earle referred with regret to the absence of Commissioner Colman from the meeting, which was the more painful since he was detained by the recent death of his mother and the sickness of Mrs. C. He also introduced the paper of Captain G. Doppelmair, of Kiev, Russia, but as it had not been translated it could not be read.
NOTE.—The Secretary has since had the paper translated through the kindness of Mr. Tuisco Greiner, of New Jersey, which is here presented." - Pg 120 -....

In 1889, Tuisco and his growing family returned to New York.

March 1889- *Naples Record*

"Mrs. Tuisco Greiner and her daughters, Mary and Zora are spending a few days with relatives here."

The residents of Naples, including family – may not have been ready to welcome Tuisco back in their midst. My guess is that, while *Mrs.* Tuisco Greiner and the girls were representing the family, in Naples, *Mr.* Tuisco Greiner and his sons were busy settling their new home and farm, in the boom town of Niagara, New York.

Chapter Eight

La Salle and Family Life

"The madam seems to enjoy these walks for observation just as much as I do – of course to expect her to have her eye entirely closed to my many imperfections is almost asking too much of the good woman."

The Garden Book for Practical Farmers 1901 - Pg. 30

Cora Bartholomew Greiner
"The Good Woman"

After Hester's death from typhoid, in 1892, it was believed that the well water was contaminated, so the family moved from their home in Niagara Falls to La Salle, Niagara, NY, where, in daughter Helma's words, her father "had use of the farm by acting as caretaker. The owner was a man named Long, who was the son-in-law of Harold Bell Wright."

After doing some research, I discovered that "the man named Long" was editor Elias A. Long 1849-1917. He was Harold Bell Wright's father-in-law, not his son-in-law, as Helma had thought. Harold was the author of popular Western novels, from which many classic western movies were made.

Elias A. Long House
La Salle, Niagara, NY - Overlooking Cayuga Creek

Picture from Helma Greiner Merrill's
"Down Memory Lane"

Tuisco was left a widower with three young children and a young niece to manage the household and to care for the children.

TUISCO GREINER

It seemed inevitable…

September 5, 1894- *Naples Record*

"Married – Greiner – Bartholomew – At La Salle, N.Y. August 28, 1894 by Rev. Mr. Warner, Tuisco Greiner of La Salle, and Miss Cora E. Bartholomew of Naples.

Mr. and Mrs. Tuisco Greiner of La Salle, N.Y. are spending their honeymoon among relatives in town."

Forty-eight-year-old Tuisco had married his 26-year-old niece (in-law). Cora was 22 years younger than her husband. When the story was told by family members they would say, "I'm not sure, but I think she was his first wife's sister." Maybe they really didn't know, or maybe they just didn't feel quite comfortable saying she married her much older Uncle (in-law).

Cora and Tuisco also had four children together. All were born in La Salle, NY – Albin in 1896, Paul, 1898, Guido, 1900 and Helma in 1905.

Tuisco & Cora (Bartholomew) Greiner Family

On the left: Helma 1, Cora 37, Paul 7
On the right: Tuisco 59, Guido 4, Albin 9

(Regrettably, a picture of Tuisco with his first family – Hester, Mary, Zora, Louis and Otto, was not available.)

"The Good Woman"

Cora – In Her Daughter's Words:

"My mother saw that we went to Sunday School every Sunday. We went to the Methodist Church which was on the other side of the tracks. It was quite a walk. I joined the church when I was eight years old. I don't remember my mother going to church very often. She went on special occasions, such as Christmas, when the children put on programs. I know she was a good Christian woman and was very concerned about her family. We went a few times to the Lutheran Church, the denomination my father belonged to.

Our Sunday School usually had a picnic every summer. We would take sandwiches and take the trolley to Niagara Falls and eat on the grass. How different things are at the falls now. Once we crossed the bridge to Canada. We took the trolley on the Canadian side. When we got on, my mother turned the seat back and held the hand of a blind boy sitting behind her. We rode along the river and went down some steps to a park near the river."

Helma Greiner Merrill, Down Memory Lane 1992

Cora - In Her Husband's Words

"...The occasion when my madame comes out in the garden, ready for a walk through the various vegetable patches, are common, very common indeed. It's during spring, summer and fall an almost daily occurrence, but none the less valued for all that. The madam seems to enjoy these walks for observation just as much as I do – of course to expect her to have her eye entirely closed to my many imperfections is almost asking too much of the good woman."

The Garden Book for Practical Farmers 1901 - Pg. 30

Tuisco may not have been the perfect husband or father, as he readily admitted in his writings, but I do know that his youngest daughter, Helma, adored him. She was only 9 years old when both of her parents died, so, what memories she had of them were so precious to her.

Tuisco – In His Daughter's Words

Helma wrote about her father's love for music – one that inspired her own love of the piano and organ. She remembered him playing, on the piano, the music he'd heard after attending a concert, and at other times he would play new songs that she'd never heard before. When she asked what the name of the song was, her father just answered, "I haven't named it, yet."

Christmastime

"We had a regular German Christmas. We never saw our tree until Christmas morning. My father put it up after we had gone to bed. It was lighted with candles and under the tree it was divided off for oranges, candies, nuts, etc. The tree was on a table and looked very tall. Probably if I saw it today, it wouldn't look so tall. I remember one Christmas morning, I got a table with two chairs, a set of dishes, a doll and more. I still have the table.… I also had a letter from Santa Claus saying that if I didn't behave better, I wouldn't get anymore presents."

Helma Greiner Merrill, Down Memory Lane 1992

One morning she woke to the sound of paper rustling in her room. She opened her eyes, and was surprised to find that her father had returned from one of his trips and was gently unwrapping tissue paper from a box with a new "baby doll" in it for her. She didn't have it for very long…

"When I went to Aunt Grace's to live, I didn't take it with me. I dreamed many times of going back to look for it."

Helma Greiner Merrill, Down Memory Lane 1992

To make things worse, nine-year-old Helma was not allowed to go into her father's office, after his death, to take the things that she loved the most about him – the things that would have helped keep him alive, and close by, in her mind and heart. Among them were the songs he had written, and many pictures of the children in the garden with their father. She was told they had been "destroyed".

At The Dinner Table

"…if the reader has never been bountifully provided with good celery, or has never observed "confirmed celery eaters" "at work", I wish he could see the quantities of this vegetable that are brought upon my table, and notice the keen enjoyment with which all members of my family take hold of the crisp stalks. I would not miss the privilege of having a full home supply…."

Celery for Profit 1893 – pg. 12

"I and my family live almost exclusively on the product of garden and poultry yard during the entire summer, and we enjoy pretty good health generally. No meat bills to pay, no nausea caused by greasy food, no dyspepsia!"

How To Make The Garden Pay 1890 - Pg. 14

When I first read this, I had to laugh. I had the privilege of hearing this wonderful and somewhat stern advice, almost word for word, from my Grandmother's own mouth as she stood by the kitchen table watching me cook a hot, heavy, meaty meal on a warm summer day. Youthful ignorance…

Family Health

"The stomach, therefore is the pivotal point around which all the rest revolves. Put proper food into a normal stomach and the result will be good blood, and consequently mental, physical and moral health."

"The marked influence of diseased conditions of blood and stomach was shown quite convincingly to me in a recent case in my own family. We have a little fellow who was born with a slight, but very common and easily curable, defect in some important bodily functions, resulting in the retention of waste matter which seemed to vitiate the blood. When he was about a year old he began to have sudden, periodical fits of a decidedly epileptic character. To describe what frightfully vicious disposition the child developed during this time I have no words strong enough. Whenever he discovered anything that we did not want him to do, he was sure to do it, and his very aim seemed to be to do evil. If he could hurt others, he did not care how much he was hurt himself. Kindness and harsh words were alike unavailing. One can not (sic) go so far as to kill a child in order to subdue it and its evil tendencies. I was more worried about this matter; I was frightened. Where did such a disposition come from? There was good stock on both parental sides.

Finally the true cause of all the trouble was revealed to us. A slight surgical operation removed the original defect. We took pains to keep the child's stomach right, kidneys and bowels in free working order, and as the poison was gradually eliminated from his system, the fits ceased and the disposition became more and more tractable until it reached that condition which we find in the normal child. All the former viciousness of temper has disappeared; and while he still possesses the natural mischievous inclinations of the average child, his disposition is not materially different from that of the other people's children. But just let his stomach get out of order, or his bowels and kidneys refuse to perform their proper functions freely, and traces of the former viciousness of temper will at once reappear."

—*The Garden Book for Practical Farmers* (1901) Pgs. 20-21

Good old fashioned, sound advice that never goes out of style! We all should heed, but too many of us struggle to follow.

Chapter Nine

The "Doughty Reformer"

"Warrant Sworn Out for the Doughty La Salle Reformer this morning and case will be Heard Before Judge Tomkins on Tuesday night… Through the streets of the Village the news spread. Mr. Greiner is a justice in the village and a reform advocate."

May 29, 1908 - *Niagara Falls Gazette*

Tuisco had moved his family from Little Silver, NJ to La Salle, Niagara County, NY. in 1889. The town of La Salle was originally part of the town of Niagara until it officially became a village in 1897, then in 1927, it was annexed to the city of Niagara Falls. A quote on niagarafrontier.com gives us an idea of the conditions in the area at the time Tuisco moved his family there:

"In 1889, the Cataract Construction Company was incorporated in New Jersey. This company created a large new mill region encompassing 1,580 acres on a two-mile tract of land located upstream of the Reservation State Park and the Falls"

I don't know what prompted Tuisco to move his family to La Salle. I imagine, as an author, he may have been acquainted with the editor, Elias A. Long, and perhaps heard that his farm was available to rent. It would be the perfect place for his business - and closer to Naples, and the family they must have sorely missed. There were other Greiners in the Buffalo area at that time, but none that I was able to link to Tuisco. In any case, the Niagara Falls area was booming with new businesses, and with it, the usual rough characters following in the midst of the family men looking to profit, or just looking for whatever work they could get.

I do know that with Tuisco's exuberant sense of justice, he was a natural candidate for political office, and true to form - not without controversy.

Village Board of Trustees

November 27, 1911-*Niagara Falls Gazette*
THREATENS INJUNCTION TO
PREVENT BIG EXPENDITURE
Should Tax Election in La Salle Carry This Afternoon Courts Will Be Appealed to in Effort to Stop Bonding of Village

"That the situation in the village of La Salle, with regard to the proposition to bond the municipality for $270,000 for public improvements, is anything but harmonious, is evidenced by the threat that is heard today to the effect that in the vent of the success of the courts in an effort to prevent the expenditure of the money. The polls in the village opened at 2 o'clock this afternoon and will close at 8 o'clock this evening. The issue is in doubt as the elements for and against the proposition seem to be pretty evenly divided. Tuisco Greiner, a member of the village board of trustees, is one of the leading residents of the village who is opposed to the idea of saddling the big expense upon the community. "I am not an obstructionist," said Mr. Greiner this morning, "and I believe in having all the improvements that are going, but there is no sense in saddling the village with such a burden when these things can be better left to private enterprise, which would give us a much better service in the end. We have very few men in the village capable of managing such a tremendous enterprise, and with the small amount of time even they would give it, we would be in a pretty mess very shortly.

More than this, the people of the village are now complaining of the burden of carrying the school bond burden. It is proposed to pay off the first installment of the $270,000 in five years, which would mean a large tax, ten dollars or more, for every man, woman and child in the village. It is no wonder people are trying to dispose of their property and leave the village. The taxes are becoming prohibitive.

If this election carries I shall appeal to the courts to prevent bonding the village. I shall ask for an unjunction restraining the village Board on the ground that notice of the election was not sufficient, and that only five days before the election did we receive the prospectus, which was altogether too short a time to study the figures. I do not believe those who are advocationg the expenditure fully realize what it means. They look for the village to advance by leaps and bounds by reason of these improvements, but I do not share their optimism."

Justice of the Peace - Run for Assembly

September 27, 1901-*Lockport Journal*
DEMOCRATS NOMINATE
Second Assembly District ConTentlon—Tuisco Greiner Named for Assembly.

"The Democratic convention for the second assembly district was held in the village of Wilson this afternoon. The convention was called to order by D. Gurney Spalding, the chairman of the Democratic County Committee. The convention was permanently organized with Frederick Chormann of Niagara Falls, as chairman, and E. T. Williams, of Niagara Falls, as secretary. J. W. H. Kelly of Lewiston and John A. Landrigan of Niagara Falls were chosen tellers. The usual resolutions were passed. The convention nominated Tuisco Greiner of La Salle, for member of assembly. Greiner is a justice of the peace of the town of Niagara."

It appears from the following that Tuisco was not considered a serious contender, but at least he had the courage to try:

September 28, 1901 - *Lockport Journal*

"PERFORMED A DUTY ANYWAY. The Democrats of the second assembly district made their assembly nomination on Friday. They nominated a man who may be pretty well known in his own immediate neighborhood, but has been heard of but little, if at all, in this end of the county. Tuisco Greiner, a country justice of the peace, has been accorded the honor of contesting the coming election in the second district with the Republican nominee, the Hon. John H. Leggett. That is about all the honor Mr. Tuisco Greiner will be likely to get out of his campaign. We doubt if the men who nominated him, even, expect that he will be able to come out of the fight with any showing of strength. It looks like a case of leading someone to the sacrifice and of taking Mr. Tuisco Greiner because he may have been willing and because no one else may have cared to stand against the popular Republican nominee. Mr. Tuisco Greiner will no doubt enjoy some measure of importance in the political arena at the start, but when the votes are counted on election night he is likely to disappear at an early stage of the interesting proceeding. Our friend Leggett of the second district has reason to be pretty well satisfied with the kindly manner in which the Democrats of his district seem to have been playing into his hands."

Business was definitely booming in Niagara Falls! Numerous grain mills and the power company were vying for space to build on the river, digging canals and tunnels to harness the massive water power.

It didn't take long before utility vs. preservation of the beautiful Falls became an issue.

August 18, 1906 - *Rural New Yorker*
"THE DESTROYING OF NIAGARA FALLS."
By Tuisco Greiner

"On page 589 Mr. McFarland speaks of the "plain people of the country" who come to see the Falls because they love the Falls, and are uplifted and benefitted by viewing God's majesty as there displayed. In fact, the great majority of the plain people who visit the Falls go there just as they would go to a picnic, or to a circus – for a day's outing or out of curiosity, and they would be uplifted and benefitted just as much as going to the seashore – or to any pleasure resort. In all creation the predominance of the utilitarian spirit can be recognized. I cannot imagine that a kind and all-wise Providence has created the great cataracts and rushing waters of the world just for the sake of their circus show features. When hungry humanity asks for bread, the great Creator does not hang up the rich loaves in a show case, does he? "You look so far, so much a look, but you must not touch!" I cannot look at the Falls without being uplifted and inspired. Hidden in the great mass of waters I see a vast amount of human comfort and happiness —warmth and light for the homes of millions, and rest for their tired muscles, and my heart is overflowing with faith and hope and new courage and gratitude. Were not these waters made to flow and jump so as to minister to the wants and necessities of a needy people? Did the All-Wise and Almighty not foresee that a time would come when the supply of wood on the earth's surface would run short and the greedy claws of Avarice under the claim of "divine right" would have clutched the vast deposits of coal and oil in the bowels of the earth, exacting every drop of sweat and blood that can be squeezed out of the "plain people?" The day may not be far when the plain people will demand their rightful inheritance, theirs by divine right in fact, and take the management of their affairs in their own hands. Having lost control of the coal and the oil, they demanded and secured free alcohol, which may turn out a competitor to coal and oil, and they should try to make such use of the waters that Providence has put within their reach and will inure the benefits to the plain people rather than as at present to a few favored corporations whom the new law is trying to give a monopoly. As a matter of fact, the destruction of the Falls and its scenic beauty, even if all the present demands of the power companies are acceded to, seems to be a long way off. The changes that have thus far taken place have enhanced rather than marred the scenic beauty of the Falls and added to the interest that attaches to its various features."

Despite Tuisco's forthright and sometimes abrasive ways, his heart was in the right place. He cared deeply for the common man, as we learn clearly from his writings. Thank God for those who speak up when they see or perceive social injustice!

Run for Re-election as President of La Salle
SATURDAY, MARCH 7, 1908, *NIAGARA FALLS GAZETTE.*
LA SALLE ELECTORS IN CAUCUS TODAY
Tuisco Greiner Has Been Eliminated.—Republican Ticket Will Be a Winner.

"The electors of the village of La Salle are holding their caucuses this afternoon. The Republicans started at 8 o'clock, and the Democrats at 1 o'clock. The Republican polls will close at 7 o'clock and the Democrat polls at 8 o'clock. The indications point to the nomination of Fred Brooks for president by the Republicans, and of George Greenwaldt by the Democrats. President Tuisco Greiner appears to be eliminated. He Is not in favor with his party, and his recent action in regard to the electric light question has estranged many of his Republican friends. It is a foregone conclusion that William Gombert and E. P. Bowen Will be re-nominated by the Republicans as trustees. The Democrats are expected to name Ferdinand Strassburg and Fred Hartmann for those offices. H. C Kinsey will be re-nominated by the Republicans for treasurer."

With any boom town, there usually come the humble family men as well as the rowdy dudes looking for a good paying job in the dirty, backbreaking work of Boom Town construction. Guns were readily available for protection and law enforcement – and Tuisco did not hesitate to use one when he believed justice was being compromised…

Yes, he did….

May 29, 1908 - *Niagara Falls, NY Gazette*
Justice Greiner Draws Gun on Saloon Keeper
Ejected When He Complained of Violation

"Warrant Sworn Out for the Doughty La Salle Reformer this morning and case will be Heard Before Judge Tomkins on Tuesday night.

Tuisco Greiner former president of the village of La Salle, was arrested this morning about 3'oclock at his home in Creek Road by Constable Frank Knight on a warrant, issued to Albert L Grose, saloon keeper, by Justice of the Peace, H.S. Tomkins.

Through the streets of the Village the news spread. Mr. Greiner is a justice in the village and a reform advocate.

He was charged with pointing a revolver at Grose and threatening to shoot. This Greiner admitted to a Gazette reporter, claiming however, that it was self-defense.

The trouble took place at Grose's Saloon, The Niagara Café in Main street about 1 o'clock this morning. Grose recently bought the saloon, and last night he held an opening and 'twas an opening. At midnight the door was locked, so Grose alleges that and only a few friends in the saloon were served with drinks.

Justice Greiner called at the side door of the saloon shortly after midnight to stop an alleged fight, information of which he had received over the telephone, he said. Grose was accused of violation of the excise law. Words and compliments were freely exchanged and Justice Greiner was ordered from the place by the proprietor.

He was followed to the walk, he alleges, and was about to be attacked by the proprietor and his friends, when he pulled the shooting iron. "Stand back or I'll shoot," he shouted. The Justice left the place and went home.

After his departure, a warrant was issued for his arrest. Greiner, it is said, was in bed when the constable called.

The case was to have been tried in the town Hall at 10 o'clock this morning, but on request of Greiner it was adjourned until next Tuesday night at 8 o'clock.

Greiner was released on his own recognizance. The villagers, both men and women flocked to the town Hall to hear the case. Remarks were freely made by those present that they did not want any "gun play" in the village, while others advocated abolishing the saloons."

I have to admit, I get a chuckle out of this article, when I think of my 3-year-old Grandmother sleeping snug in her bed, while her beloved father was out protecting the citizens of La Salle from the rowdy crowds. It does sound humorous today, and apparently, the writer of the article thought so, too.

Even so, I am still amazed at this, my great-Grandfather. He kept that exuberance of spirit and love of justice all his life, even after a brief, but disastrous fall from grace in Naples. I wonder if he ever thought of that time? I wonder if he sometimes sat at home with his head in his hands, chastising himself for having brought so much trouble to his family and friends. Did that memory drive him in his career as Town Justice – to redeem himself?

The newspapers were not always kind to Tuisco, and yet, he wasn't afraid to pull himself out of the pit of scandal and to keep trying. He wasn't afraid to be a "character" if it got the job done. He wasn't afraid of being the "Doughty Reformer".

A few days later, we learn the logical outcome of the story:

June 1, 1908 - *Niagara Falls Gazette*
A TRUCE IN LA SALLE.

"A truce has been struck In La Salle between the reform element and the saloon men. The latter have promised to behave in the future and to rigidly observe the law. In consideration of which the reformers will not rush pending proceedings. The compromise, which Is distinctly, a victory for law and order, came about after the somewhat sensational episode of Thursday night last when Justice T. Greiner personally appeared at a saloon where the law was being violated in the dispensing of liquors after hours, and demanded the place be closed. Greiner was arrested for drawing a revolver, but the saloonkeeper will not push that charge, for in the reckoning, the doughty Justice, it Is generally admitted, would have much the better of it. All that is desired is that the saloons be conducted in an orderly and decent manner, and when thus mindful of the law, they will not be molested."

Less than two weeks later…

Oh, the Many and Varied Roles of the Justice of the Peace…

June 10, 1908—*Niagara Falls Gazette*

HAS ANYONE LOST A LITTLE POLISH GIRL?

"Whoever has lost a little ten-year old Polish girl had better get to La Salle as soon as possible and call on Peace Justice Tuisco Greiner. The little girl was found wandering about the outskirts of the village early this afternoon, weeping her tear wells dry. She was perfectly well, but dreadfully hungry. She won't stop crying, she says, until she is properly found by her parents. So please hurry."

February 27, 1909 - *The Buffalo Express*
TUISCO GREINER TO RUN AGAIN?

"If not as a regular Democrat, he will probably be independent Candidate."

FOR LA SALLE IS ROUSED

"Some of the Villagers don't like handling of lighting Extension and handling of Liquor Question.
Niagara Falls, February 26 – The annual election in the village of La Salle will be held on Tuesday, March 16th. The time for the caucuses will be determined at a meeting of the board of trustees to be held next Monday night. Nominations must be filed with the village clerk no later than March 8th.
There is more than the usual interest in the forthcoming election because of the vital issues which have been presented during the administration of President Greenwald.

A considerable party of villagers do not like the way the president and the board have handled the lighting situation and there is some opposition to the way in which the present administration has dealt with the liquor question.

It is not at all unlikely that Tuisco Greiner, if he is not regularly nominated by the democrats, will again run independently. James G. T (unreadable) is a likely candidate for the nomination for president. President Greenwald is again in the field for the democratic nomination."

March 18, 1909—*North Tonawanda Evening News*
LA SALLE DEMOCRATS ELECTED PRESIDENT

"…The Republicans feel sure that if Tuisco Greiner had not injected himself independently into the field they would have elected their ticket from top to bottom. The erstwhile Democrat drew enough votes away from the Republican ticket to upset affairs…"

Chapter Ten

Heartbreak and Tragedy

"(Her) life was beautiful as the morning rays, pure as the noontide splendor and mild as the breath of evening. Too pure for earth, she passed away, like the flower that withers and dies in an uncongenial clime."

Hester (Bartholomew) Greiner's Obituary 1892
(Original source: "Christian Diadem and Family Keepsake 1856, Vol 6")

Standing: Elizabeth Bartholomew Pulver, Cora and Tuisco (Elizabeth was Cora's Aunt, and sister to Tuisco's first wife) Front: Georgia, Alice, Carrie, (Gotthold's daughters), Zora, Helma (Tuisco's daughters), Flora (Cora's sister)

It seems the Greiner Brothers were known as much for their tragedies, as they were for their successful business ventures. I chose to list them all in one chapter so the reader could have a good cry all at once and avoid casting a pall over the entire book.

It's hard to imagine one family experiencing so many near deaths and horrific losses – it would seem too much to bear. There is nothing I can say that would tell their stories any better than what was written before me…

1880 Brother Gotthold came very close to being the first Greiner casualty in Naples -

January 8, 1880 - *The Neapolitan*

"A few days since C. G, Greiner had a hair-breadth escape which should be a warning to all who are at work in the woods. A tree had been felled on the side hill opposite Seymour Wheeler's and had been trimmed preparatory to being moved down the incline; Mr. Greiner took a cant hook in his hand, went to the body of the huge log, only a few feet from the butt, to assist in starting it, but it started by his touch, throwing the lever of the hook violently against his breast, and landing him, fortunately, upon the log; he was carried down about three rods when the butt of the tree plowed into a hillock and stopped; he was unconscious by the blow, and when the tree stopped he rolled off and slid down with his head against the same hillock. Two others were near by who cared for him, and no serious results followed his narrow escape from death."

1888 Gotthold and Tuisco's father in-law would die of blood poisoning –

January 18 1888 - *Naples Record*

"Mrs. Tuisco Greiner, of Little Silver, N, J., is at Garlinghouse caring for her father, Aaron Bartholomew, who is dangerously ill with blood poison."

January 20 1888 - *Ontario County Journal*

"Naples, N. Y. - Aaron Bartholomew, an old and prominent resident of Garlinghouse, in this town, died on Tuesday at the age of 78 years. Some two weeks since, his grandson pared a corn upon the toe of his grandfather, and shaved so closely that the blood flowed. Blood poisoning from this slight cause has resulted in his death."

January 20, 1888 - Garlinghouse

"Tuisco Greiner came up from Little Silver, N, J. on Friday last to attend the funeral of Mr. Bartholomew."

Less than two months later:

1888 - Brother Luie's son, Paul Greiner, was killed –

January 20, 1888 - *Naples Record,* Garlinghouse

"Paul Greiner, late from Germany, arrived here on Friday last. He is stopping with his uncles, the Greiner Bros."

TUISCO GREINER

March 7, 1888 Garlinghouse - *Naples Record*

"On Wednesday of last week, G.C. and Paul Greiner were cutting logs upon the farm of S.J. Merrill. They had just cut down a tree and as it was falling they looked for falling limbs, but none were to be seen as all was clear overhead, but before the tree reached the ground it came in contact with a tall slim beech and bent it over well toward the ground. When it sprung back to its upright position it brought a limb from the falling tree top, about three inches through and ten or twelve feet long, throwing it at least forty feet high in the air and then it fell near the stump of the tree just cut, striking Paul against the right side of the head, crushing the skull in a very frightful manner. Fortunately, help was near at hand who carried him to the house of G.C. Greiner but by the time they reached the house, life was extinct. Mr. Greiner came from Germany last October, intending to make this his future home. He was 18 years of age and a cabinet maker by trade. He was a man of fine attainments, mild, kind, affectionate. He was fast learning our language and our ways of working, and he enjoyed it all so much. He was buoyant and happy and looked into the future with fond hopes and bright anticipations; little realizing that he was so soon to be stricken down. It is seldom, if ever, a heavier blow has fallen upon this community. All both old and young, lament his most untimely death and mourn and sympathize with his brothers and sisters at home, and we hope and pray God's grace may sustain and comfort them in this the saddest bereavement of their lives. A very large concourse of people attended his funeral on Saturday, March 10, 1888, the Rev. J.H. Masten officiating. He quietly sleeps in our cemetery here."

(Family lore tells us that Paul's family in Germany reported hearing the unexplained sound of a falling tree around the same time that Paul had died.)

1889 Cora's father, William Bartholomew, would die of gangrene –

(William was also brother-in-law to Gotthold by his wife Jane and to Tuisco by his first wife Hester.)

September 13, 1889 - *Ontario County Journal*

"Naples, N. Y. - The death of Wm. Bartholomew was sad and excited much sympathy. He was thrown from his wagon two months ago in a runaway and his leg was injured. He suffered a great deal with it, but did not realize its condition until a week ago. Dr. Parker was called in and found the leg rotten. It had evidently been neglected.

Dr. Beahan, of Canandaigua, was consulted and amputation was decided upon. On Thursday the operation was performed, but it was too late, and the poor man died Friday morning. The deceased was highly esteemed; was a hard-working, honest man; had a large family; was elected town collector last spring. By arduous army service his constitution had been weakened. An immense number of friends attended his funeral at his home in Garlinghouse on Sunday."

In 1891, each of the Greiner brothers would lose a child –

February – Friedemann's little firstborn, Bessie, died.

February 18, 1891 - *Naples Record*

"A VERY sad death was that of little Bessie P., only child of Mr. and Mrs. Friedeman Greiner. Bessie was a lovely, stout little girl of three years, charming in person and manner. She was taken with pneumonia about four weeks ago, but had nearly recovered from that severe illness, when inflammation of the bowels set in, and lacking strength to resist the last disease, died on Friday. The funeral was on Sunday afternoon at the house. There was real, deep sorrow and genuine sympathy for the bereaved parents on the part of each one of the very large number of friends who were present. Rev. Mr. Sanborn drew from the Word of God thoughts that were very comforting, but in the presence of that beautiful form cold in death grief would have its sway. The little casket was covered with flowers, but none so sweet as the blossom within, now transplanted to a fairer clime."

Only two Months later:

April - Gotthold's only son, Charley, died of Typhoid Fever –

April 15, 1891- *Naples Record*

"Charley, only son of G. C. Greiner, departed this life April 8, aged 20 years and 9 months. Charley was of a bright, sprightly, pleasing disposition, the joy and pride of his fond, loving parents' hearts. In him their full hopes and expectations were centered, but now he is gone. Their hopes are blighted, their expectations ruined. In society he was a general favorite, loved and respected by all. He was a faithful worker in the Sunday School where for years he had labored earnestly for its welfare and in all public and private enterprises he has stood in the front. His spotless reputation we revere; his memory we cherish. His funeral was largely attended on Friday, April 10, by Rev. J. H. Masten, assisted by a choir, G. C. Deyo, E. C. Clark, Mrs. Hattie Caulkins and Mrs. Frank Lewis, of Naples. His remains were interred in our cemetery here."

August 24, 1891 - *Naples Record*

"Last Spring the Garlinghouse Sunday school suffered a great loss in the death of Charley Greiner. He was a willing worker, and ever ready to take any position, or to do any work assigned him. His kind, genial disposition won him many friends. The school wishing to show their appreciation of his worth and their sympathy with the afflicted family, raised money to purchase some flowers to be placed upon his casket. The flowers were ordered, but from some cause were not received. Now they have taken the money and purchased a very fine crayon portrait of Charley, and last Sunday through the superintendent, presented the picture to Charley's parents, Mr. and Mrs. G.C. Greiner."

Nine months after cousin Charley died:

Tuisco and Hester's first born, died –

December 30, 1891 - *Naples Record*

"Mr. and Mrs. G.C. Greiner were called to La Salle Niagara co., yesterday morning to care for their niece, Miss Mary Greiner who is critically ill."

December 30, 1891 - *Niagara Falls Gazette*
Miss Mary Greiner

"Miss Mary Greiner died at the home of her parents, Mr. and Mrs. T. Greiner, at La Salle, Tuesday morning, of typhoid fever. Although death was not wholly unexpected it was a great shock to her large circle of friends inasmuch as hopes for her recovery were expressed until just before she expired. The case is especially sad considering how keenly the loss will be felt by the host of friends her sweet nature had won. Although young she was enthusiastically engaged in all Sunday school matters. To her parents the blow is a sad one. She was the object of their hopes and ambitions. Miss Mary Greiner was born at Naples, N Y., on the 12 of October, 1872, the eldest of four children. The funeral will occur Thursday afternoon from her home at La Salle. Interment will be near Naples."

Dec. 31, 1891 - *Rochester Democrat and Chronicle*

"Western New York News - Steuben County - Miss Mary Greiner, aged 19 years died at her home in La Salle Tuesday morning after a protracted illness. She was the eldest daughter of Tuisco Greiner, formerly of Naples. Her remains will be brought to Bloods*

to-day and the funeral held at the residence of her grandmother, Mrs. Ann BARTHOLOMEW, in Garlinghouse, to-morrow morning, Rev. J. H. MASTEN officiating."
*Now Atlanta, NY

Less than two weeks after Mary died, Tuisco's mother would be gone:

January 1892 - Germany

"Caroline Naeter Greiner died at age 80, in Germany. She probably never had the chance to meet her American grandchildren, or daughters-in-law."

Hester and Tuisco's niece, Cora Bartholomew would stay with the family, while they mourned and healed. She must have been such a comfort to them.

A Healing Pause:

May 25, 1892 - *Naples Record*

"Tuisco Greiner spent a portion of last week here and with his brother, G.C. Greiner, did some very commendable work on their lot in the cemetery here, which says to us, "Go Thou and do likewise." (Luke 10:37)

1892 NYS Census Niagara, Niagara, NY –

Tuisco Greiner, aged 46, Editor, Hester 42, Zora 17, Luie 13, Otto 5, Cora Bartholomew 24

August 9, 1892 – Garlinghouse - *Naples Record*

"Miss Cora Bartholomew, who has been at La Salle for the past six months, returned home on Saturday.

Mrs. Tuisco Greiner (Hester) of La Salle is visiting her mother, Mrs. Ann Bartholomew, and other relatives for a few days."

1891 had come and mercifully, had gone, but no one could predict, or even imagine the horrendous grief that still lay ahead.

Four months after Hester's visit to Naples, and almost exactly a year after Mary's death:

1892 - Tuisco's wife, Hester Bartholomew Greiner died –

December 1892 – Garlinghouse - *Naples Record*

"The many friends of Mrs. Tuisco Greiner are pained to learn that she is lying very low with fever at her home in La Salle, N.Y."

December 19, 1892 – Garlinghouse - *Naples Record*
"In Memoriam"

"On Thursday morning last, our community was startled by the sad intelligence that Mrs. Tuisco Greiner was dead. It seemed almost incredible that one who only a few days before was enjoying such good health, so strong, so robust, and with such fair prospects of living to a good old age, so suddenly be called away.

Hester Bartholomew was born in Garlinghouse December 15, 1850. Her girlhood days and in fact nearly her whole life had been spent in our midst. We all knew her but to love and respect her. Being of an unusually mild temperament from early youth she became a general favorite with all her associates, an ornament to society, and an honor to herself, her family and to the community in which she moved. We mourn her as my sister, my companion, and my friend, whose *life was beautiful as the morning rays, pure as the noontide splendor and mild as the breath of evening. Too pure for earth, she passed away, like the flower that withers and dies in an uncongenial clime.* She was married to Tuisco Greiner in 1872. Their union was blessed by two bright boys, and two lovely daughters, Mary, the eldest died nearly a year ago and the others survive her, and mourn the loss of a mother. Her sickness was short and of such a mild, but deceptive character that no special fears of her recovery were entertained until the day before her death when hemorrhage set in, which soon closed her early career. From the first of her sickness she felt the consciousness that she should not recover, and gave the most positive assurance that she was fully prepared and ready to go at the call of the Master to enjoy those fairer and happier climes above. After appropriate religious services at the home, her remains were brought here to the home of her mother, Mrs. Ann Bartholomew, where on Saturday, December 17, a funeral service was held, by Rev, J.H. Masten assisted by D.A. Parcelly officiating. A large concourse of friends and neighbors came to sympathize and mourn with the afflicted ones and to pay the last tribute of respect to one who in life they held so dear. Her remains were interred in our cemetery here."

December 19, 1892 – Garlinghouse - *Naples Record*

"A number of acquaintances attended the funeral of Mrs. Tuisco Greiner, Rome Clason and wife and Mrs. Sidney Merrill attended the funeral of their cousin, Mrs. Greiner last Saturday at Garlinghouse. She died in La Salle, recently."

Within a year, the three most important and beloved women in Tuisco's life were gone.

There would be a twelve-year reprieve before the next (known) tragedy would strike the Greiner Brother's family, in the meantime, Tuisco came very close to losing his own life:

June 10, 1902 - *North Tonawanda Evening News*

"Tuisco Greiner of La Salle was the Democratic Candidate for Member of Assembly in the second district last fall, had a narrow escape from drowning in the Niagara River near La Salle yesterday. His boat which carried a small sail overturned and Greiner saved himself by clinging to the capsized craft. He was rescued by another sailing party."

1904 Gotthold would lose his wife, Alice Jane –

March 2, 1904 - *Naples Record*

"Perry Bartholomew and his sister Mrs. Elizabeth Pulver spent last week with their sister Mrs. Charles Greiner at La Salle, NY, who is in a very precarious state of health. Mrs. Pulver remained to care for Mrs. Greiner, Mr. Bartholomew returning Saturday."

April 3, 1904 - *Niagara Falls Gazette*

"Mrs. G. C. Greiner, a well known and respected resident of the town of Niagara died on Tuesday at the family home on the Lake Rd. She was 60 years of age and is survived by a husband and family. The funeral will be observed tomorrow and interment will be made in Tonawanda."

May 18, 1904 - *Naples Record*
In Memoriam.

"Jane Bartholomew was born in Garlinghouse November 25, 1846, and died of cancer of the stomach at her home in LaSalle, N. Y. April 28,1904. Deceased was one of a family of eight children born to Aaron and Ann Bartholomew, of whom but one sister, Mrs. W. L. Pulver, and two brothers, David and Perry Bartholomew, of Naples, survive. In the winter of 1868 she was united in marriage with Mr. G. C. Greiner, and had always resided in Naples until about eight years ago when they removed to LaSalle, where they have since resided and where she died. To them six children were born, of whom three daughters, Mrs. M. Goodrich and Misses Georgia and Allie

Greiner, together with the husband, survive her, and mourn the loss of a most affectionate companion and a kind, loving mother. Mrs. Greiner consecrated herself to Christ during the winter of 1864-65, under the pastoral labors of Reverends Duncan and Peck, and soon after united with the M. E. church of Garlinghouse, of which she has since been a most efficient and acceptable member. Her life has been one of explicit trust and confidence in God, her faith has been strong and unwavering, her anticipations have been large, and her reward will be abundant. The testimony both of the family circle and neighbors is that she bore an even temper, calm, peaceful, hopeful. She had no word against anyone but sought the good of all. Though of a quiet life she had drawn to herself by her large heartedness, a large circle of friends here and elsewhere to mourn her loss, sharing with her family the grief they bear. All attest her large-hearted love, zeal, tender care in behalf of others, and her character which was completely above reproach, her agreeable disposition; her patient, sunny, encouraging spirit was an example always safe to follow. The funeral services were held from the home May 1, 1904, Rev. F. L. Wemette officiating, who gave a very interesting and appropriate discourse from 2 Cor. 5:1."

Eight years later, the Greiner family must have thought their worst nightmares were coming true. Cora would not recover from this one:

1912 Tuisco and Cora's son, Paul Greiner – Killed by a train – March 25, 1912 - *The Evening News,* North Tonawanda
La Salle Boy Killed By Central Train

"La Salle, March 25 – Paul Greiner, twelve year old son of Tuisco Greiner was struck and instantly killed on the Tompkins Crossing here Saturday, by New York Central passenger train No. 41 Falls bound. The lad attempted to run across in front of the train. Coroner Scott has the case and will hold an inquest next week."

March 27, 1912 - *Naples Record*

"Last Friday, Paul, the 14-year-old son of Tuisco Greiner, was instantly killed in La Salle, NY. He was a newsboy, and evidently confused while crossing the railroad track and was struck by the moving train, and killed. On Saturday, F. Greiner, Jesse Bartholomew, Mrs. Murray Watkins, and Mrs. David Briggs, of Naples, and John Bartholomew of Bath, Uncles and Aunts of the deceased, went to La Salle, where on Saturday, the funeral was held from the home of the parents."

Not even three months after Paul died, an article in the Niagara Gazette told the story of another incredible accident that *should have* killed Gotthold's only grandson, Carl Goodrich.

1912 - Gotthold's only grandson Carl Goodrich barely escaped death:

June 12, 1912 - *Niagara Falls Gazette*
RECEIVED FULL FORCE OF 12,000 VOLTS:
WAS SLIGHTLY INJURED

"Carl Goodrich, Employed at La Salle Lighting Station is Little Worse For His Experience Yesterday Afternoon – Hand and Both Feet Burned.

Carl Goodrich had a miraculous escape from death yesterday afternoon. Goodrich is about 20 years of age and is employed in the Power House of the Niagara Falls Gas and Electric Light company at La Salle. New machinery and equipment was recently installed in the power house and Goodrich was busy cleaning up around it when he came into contact with a live wire, receiving a shock of 12,000 volts. Few men have anything like that experience and live to tell the tale and Goodrich is congratulating himself that he is alive today.

When he realized that it takes only about 100 volts to kill some men and that only between 1,500 and 2,000 volts are used to electrocute prisoners who have been sentenced to death in Sing Sing, the remarkableness of Goodrich's escape will be the more appreciated. This morning when spoken to about the case, electrical experts said that it was the extreme voltage that saved the young man's life. They explained that just as too large a dose of poison frequently acted as an emetic so a very strong electrical shock would tend to save the life of a person who would be instantly killed by a shock of one tenth the force.

Just how the accident occurred even the young man himself does not know, but he thinks that, as he was sweeping about the machinery, he accidentally struck the loose end of a live wire with his broom, knocking it against his right hand. As he was standing on a wet concrete floor at the time the contact was thus completed and he received the full force of the shock.

But all the young Goodrich or the others who were in the power house at the time really know about the affair is that there was a flash and a report and Goodrich was hurled violently into a corner of the room where he stiffened out and fell to the floor. Fortunately for him, Chas. Barnes, superintendent of the Electric Development company of Niagara Falls, Ont., was in the building at the time of the accident, he having been in charge of the work of installing the new plant and he knew what to do and did it promptly. He quickly pulled the young man out into open space and A. H. Merritt of this city, Superintendent Allen of the La Salle plant and other employees started in to apply artificial respiration. For some time the young man's life was despaired of but after about fifteen minutes work Goodrich began to show signs of coming around and in a few minutes more he opened his eyes.

In the meantime Dr. Jayne had been summoned and when he arrived he assisted in the work of reviving the young man. After about half an hour Goodrich was able to talk, but so great had been the shock that the flesh had been burned from the finger of his right hand and his feet had also been badly burned. At first owing to the numbness following the terrible shock, he did not feel much pain, but towards evening he suffered considerably and as soon as he fully recovers from the shock it will be necessary to scraped the bones of the burned members and cut away the scorched flesh. He (his) hand and feet will likely be scarred for life, but otherwise he is not likely to suffer any ill effects from the shock.

In conversation with a Gazette representative, Goodrich said he knew little about what happened. He remembered the flash and report and then he had a number of pleasant dreams. The next thing he remembered was opening his eyes and seeing Mr. Barnes and wondering where he was and what Mr. Barnes was doing there as he had not figured in any of the dreams. It was some time before he fully regained consciousness and realized what had happened. He said that he remembered his muscles stiffening and the feeling was one that he would not care to experience again. It lasted but an instant but it seemed to him like age.

This morning outside of his burned hand and feet. Goodrich was little the worse for his experience."

1913 - Almost a year to the day after Carl was electrocuted, he looked death in the face again. This time, he just wasn't able to escape -

July 9, 1913 - *Naples Record*

"Tuesday morning's papers chronicle the drowning of five young men Sunday evening while canoeing in Lake Erie off Windmill Point. They were members of prominent families of Niagara Falls and La Salle, N.Y. Among the members was Carl Goodrich, son of Mortimer and Carrie Greiner Goodrich, former residents of Naples. The father, Mortimer Goodrich is son of Hiram Goodrich of Naples, and the mother, a daughter of Charles (Gotthold) Greiner, formerly of Naples and now of La Salle. At last accounts the body had not been recovered. The young man has many relatives here who mourn with the parents in their affliction."

July 8, 1913 - *Geneva N.Y. Daily Times*
FIVE DROWNED IN LAKE ERIE
Party Was Caught In Canoes In Fierce Gale.
FIVE OTHERS ARE SAVED

"*Buffalo, July 8* - Five young men, members of prominent families of Niagara Falls and La Salle, N.Y., were drowned on Lake Erie Sunday evening when a sudden gale overturned the canoes in which they were paddling down the lake.

The dead are: Reginald McMahon, Albert Kayner, Thomas Brophy and Edward Reichert of Niagara Falls and Carl G. Goodrich of La Salle. They ranged in age from seventeen to twenty-two years and were students in chemistry at Niagara Falls laboratories.

The party comprising ten young men in five canoes left Niagara Falls, Ontario on July 2, following the Welland River in to the Welland Canal and thence to Lake Erie. They spent Saturday and Sunday at Crystal Beach, on the Canadian shore. Early Sunday evening they left there intending to make Crescent Beach, a distance of about ten miles, before dark.

The gale caught them off Windmill Point, midway between the two beaches. Cottagers at Rose Hill first sighted the canoes battling with the waves. An alarm was sounded and several large rowboats put out to the rescue. William Cannon and Douglas McMahon the latter a brother of one of the dead boys, were first picked up. Walter Franz and Joseph Cannon were rescued by another boat."

Although the four boys, were almost exhausted, they joined the searchers after a brief rest. Franz and Cannon came upon one overturned canoe to which (George Gray was clinging feebly crying for help. He was rescued.

The search was kept up until dark and all through the night, beacon lights were kept burning along the shore. No trace of the missing five was found, however, and when one of their canoes was picked up in Niagara river yesterday, ten miles from Windmill Point, all hope was abandoned."

Around this time, numerous "For Sale" ads started showing up in the newspapers offering property and stock at increasingly lower prices. There seemed to be an urgent sense that the family had to get away from LaSalle and the grievous memory of Paul's death, as we might assume from the following ad:

May 8, 1913 – Niagara Falls Gazette

"FOR SALE—BOND AND MORTGAGE $760 on LaSalle creek property. Improved 6 per cent, 4 1/2 years to run. Cause of sale removal to western state. Inquire of T. Greiner, LaSalle, N. Y."

But, the move didn't come soon enough. Cora's health plummeted after nephew Carl's tragic death - undoubtedly, a painful reminder of her own loss, the year before. An accident during this time period was the final blow for her. Daughter Helma wrote about her mother's decline:

"In 1913, my mother began having headaches. As I remembered later, it was after she had fallen down a long flight of stairs and hit her head. We were visiting friends who lived over their grocery store and when we were leaving, she fell down the stairs… she soon was so ill that she wasn't able to get up. In October, Aunt Grace went home and took me with her. They wouldn't let me say goodbye to my mother because they thought it would upset her. They said she kept asking where her curly-headed girl was. They told her I was out playing."

Many years later, Helma asked her doctor about the symptoms her mother was having. He told her that it sounded like a possible brain tumor. It may be that Helma's memory of the fall came long after that discussion. Family members would say that Cora died of a broken heart.

TUISCO GREINER

1914 - Six months after Carl drowned, and two years after her son Paul was killed, Cora Bartholomew Greiner gave up on life:

January 28 1914 - *The Naples News*
Mrs. Tuisco Greiner

"After a long illness of nearly five months, Mrs. Cora Bartholomew, wife of Tuisco Greiner, died at her home in La Salle, NY on Wednesday, January 14, 1904 (1914). Mrs. Greiner was a daughter of the late William and Angeline Bartholomew and was born in Garlinghouse July 3, 1868. Her age was 46. She was married in August 1894 to Tuisco Greiner of La Salle and had resided there until her death. Four children were born to them, three of whom are living. Albin, Guido, Helma, and son Paul was killed by the cars two years ago. She is survived by three brothers, William of Avoca, Jesse and John of Naples, three sisters, Mrs. Murray Watkins and Mrs. David Briggs of Naples, and Mrs. D.W. Liddiard of Wayland. Funeral services were held from the home in La Salle last week Friday and the body was laid to rest in Elmlawn Cemetery. David Briggs and wife, John Bartholomew, Jesse Bartholomew and wife, Mrs. D.W. Liddiard, F. Greiner and Mrs. M.R. Watkins attended the funeral.

Mrs. Greiner was a member of the Methodist Church of Garlinghouse and later, of La Salle. She was converted early in life, and was a faithful church member, doing all that she could while in health. She was a good wife and mother. None ever entered her home without a warm welcome, nor left it without feeling the warmth of a genuine hospitality. Adhering to the faith of her fathers, she in early life united with the church and loved to attend its services when health permitted. She never rallied from the tragic death of her son, Paul. Thus the silver cord is loosed, the golden bowl is broken*, and the dirt has returned to the earth as it was, the spirit has returned to the God who gave it. *(Eccl. 12:6)"

January 14, 1939 - Niagara Falls Gazette

"THE Gazette of 25 years ago - Cora E. Greiner, wife of Justice of the Peace Tuisco Greiner, of LaSalle. She Was 45 years old and had lived in LaSalle for 22 years, during which time she had become active in the First, M. E. church and had made a large number of friends. Although she had been seriously ill only four months, members of her family said that she had never recovered from shock suffered two years previously when her young son was killed by a train. Besides her husband, she was survived by two sons, Albion (Albin) and Guido, and a daughter, Helma."

1914 After burying two wives, a daughter and a young son, Tuisco Greiner died of peritonitis, just nine months after his "good woman", Cora:

September 20, 1914 - *Buffalo Courier*
TUISCO GREINER, LA SALLE, DIES AT FALLS HOSPITAL
(Special Wire to The Courier.)

"Niagara Falls, Sept. 20 – Tuisco Greiner, peace justice at LaSalle, died at Memorial Hospital last night. Funeral will be held from his late residence on Creek road at 1 o'clock Tuesday afternoon. Burial will be in Elmlawn cemetery at Tonawanda.

Judge Greiner is survived by six children, Luis, Otto, Albin, Guido, Mrs. L. V. Luick, and Miss Helma Greiner. For some time Judge Greiner was in ill health and last Monday was operated on at the hospital. His wife died some time ago, following the tragic death of a young son, who was run down by a passenger train.

Deceased was born in Bernberg, Germany, June 16, 1846, and came to this country when twenty-three years old. He came to LaSalle in 1889."

After eight years of relative peace, three more unusually tragic deaths were left:

TUISCO GREINER

1922 Brother Friedemann Greiner, killed by his own gun –

October 1922 - American Bee Journal – Volume 62, Page 468
DEATH OF FRIEDEMANN GREINER BY ACCIDENT

"We are sorry to have to record the death of one of our good friends, who has been a contributor of the American Bee Journal since 1880. Mr. Friedemann Greiner of Naples, N.Y.

The following account, taken from a local paper, recites the accident that caused his death and gives a short biography:

DEATH OF F. GREINER

Result of Accident in Which Shotgun Was Discharged by Jar of Motor Truck

A rather unusual accident, resulting in the death of Friedemann Grieiner, of Naples, occurred on the Hunts Hollow road, about a mile from his home at an early hour Tuesday morning, August 22, 1922.

Mr. Greiner arose at about four o'clock and started with his auto truck for Allen's Hill to get some pigs, and to attend to his bees on the Honeoye Lake road en route.

At about six o'clock, Harry Freeman, on his way to work at Fred Wohlschegel's (formerly the M.M. Wheeler farm) discovered the Greiner car over the bank on the Wohlschlegel farm, and Mr. Greiner's body beside it, and hastened to the Wohlschlegel home and reported what he had found.

Mr. Wohlschlegel at once summoned relatives and neighbors by telephone and the body and car were removed to the Greiner home.

It was Mr. Greiner's habit to carry his shotgun on his frequent trips down the Hollow, and shoot woodchucks. It is supposed that the gun was standing up in the car beside him, and was jarred out, the hammer striking on the running-board and discharging the load, which entered Greiner's right side and passed upward through the lungs. Marks on the car bear out this theory. The gun was then lost from the car, and the tracks indicated that the driver lost control of the car holding the road well for several rods and then driving off the bank, where the motor stalled when a wire fence was encountered.

Mr. Greiner had lighted from the car and removed from it a canvas, apparently with the intention of spreading it upon the ground to lie upon, but fell before this could be accomplished. It is thought death must have occurred within two or three minutes after the gun exploded. Coroner Smith of Canandaigua, was notified and issued a certificate of accidental death. The car driven by Mr. Greiner did not turn over, and was not materially damaged.

Friedemann Greiner was born in Bernburg, Germany, on December 8, 1853, and came to America when about 18 years of age, since which time he had spent practically his whole life in Naples. On March 30, 1887 he was united in marriage with Miss Bertha Jennings, of Naples, who survives. Other survivors are two daughters, Mrs. H Warren Olney, of Naples, and Mrs. H. E. Shaw, of Saratoga Springs; one son, Harold Greiner of Gloversville; two brothers, G.C. Greiner, of LaSalle, NY, and one brother in Germany. Mr. Greiner was a good husband and father, and his family suffers a great loss in his genial manner and wise counsel. We feel that the community has lost a good neighbor and citizen, and extend to the bereaved family, heartfelt sympathy.

Our senior editor visited both the Greiner brothers in 1919, the older brother being G. C. Greiner, of La Salle, N. Y., who still survives.

There was much in common between F. Greiner and Mr. Dadant, for both were foreigners by birth, both had received the best of their education in foreign colleges, a classical education, including the study of the dead languages, both had come to America in their teens; both were lovers of the bee, and of similar opinions on politics and war questions, in spite of their being former dwellers of antagonistic countries.

Mr. Greiner was a practical bee-keeper of long experience. He has been for many years, secretary of the New York State Association, and of the Ontario County Beekeepers Society. He was noted for his wit and sound advice in beekeeping.

In order to show the soundness of Mr. Greiner's views in bee matters, we will reproduce in this number a short article written by him for the American Bee Journal in 1891, 31 years ago when Thos. G. Newman was still editor of this magazine..."

Just about 3 years to the day after Friedemann died:

1925 Brother Karl Gotthold Greiner was killed by a train –

Vicinity News - *The Niagara Falls Gazette*
Monday August 3, 1925

GOTTHOLD C GREINER, 83 YEARS OLD, INSTANTLY KILLED BY A PASSENGER TRAIN ON THE LA SALLE CROSSING

"Was Returning from Village and Alone at the Time; Funeral will Be Held on Wednesday Afternoon; Was Well Known Bee and Agricultural Expert.

La Salle, August 3—On Saturday evening at 7 o'clock, Gotthold C Greiner, 83 years old, No. 2605 Linden road, La Salle, was hit by a Lehigh Valley passenger train on the New York Central Cayuga Drive crossing and instantly killed. Mr. Greiner was driving his Ford run-about, which was demolished. He was alone at the time. Mr. Greiner had some business to transact at the Bank of La Salle. It was a strange coincidence that on the way down he stopped and asked George Reichert, a neighbor, if he wanted to ride to the village.

Mr. Reichert was busy in the yard of his home and declined. Mr. Greiner completed his transaction at the bank and was on his way home when the crash came. The train was headed toward the Falls and going at a high rate of speed. He failed to note Its approach and the Ford was hit squarely by the engine's fender and carried beyond the Griffon street crossing, a distance of several hundred yards. The car was completely wrecked and Mr. Greiner was dead when picked up.

Fees on Duty

Frank Fees, 65, of Tompkins street, was the flagman on duty and stated that he did everything in his power to stop Mr. Greiner's car. He carried a long pole with a stop sign attached and says he waved this frantically. The matter of gates has been discussed for this crossing on several occasions but none have been installed. It is a heavily trafficked point.

Mr. Greiner was born in Burnburgh (sic), Germany, on April 24, 1842, the son of Karl and Caroline Greiner. When he was 16 (20) years of age he came to this country alone and settled in Naples, NY. Here he engaged in the bee and agricultural business and developed one of the largest bee industries in the state. In his younger days Mr. Greiner was quite a talented musician possessing a good tenor voice and playing well on the cornet. For a number of years he played with the Myrna (sic-Myron) Sutton band of Naples, later organizing his own band known as Greiner's band.

Three Daughters Survive

Mr. Greiner was united in marriage to Alice Jane Bartholomew of Naples, and three daughters and one son were born to the couple. The son, Charlie died in 1892 when 21 years of age. The three daughters survive. They are Mrs. Mortimer Goodrich, with whom he shared his home in La Salle, Mrs. Georgia Greiner Briggs of Toledo, Ohio and Miss Alice Greiner of La Salle.

Miss Greiner is on a vacation trip and at the time of the accident was on a camping trip in Yellowstone Park. She has been located and will arrive in La Salle early Wednesday morning. Mr. Greiner attended the Methodist Episcopal church. He was a member of the—fraternal organizations.

A Bee Expert

Mr. Greiner was one of the earliest expert bee pioneers of the country. He was a steady contributor to the American Bee Journal and Gleaning's Bee Culture, Both magazines are devoted entirely to the bee industry and through his articles Mr. Greiner received hundreds of inquiries through the mails regarding bees.

Mr. Greiner was one of the grand old men of La Salle and was beloved and respected by all who knew him. He was of a sunny disposition and a general carpenter and mechanic of no mean ability He was an expert with *tools of* every description. While he was "raising money on a smaller scale during the last few years of his life, his bee farm in La Salle was a model one. It was perfect in every detail and at various times was visited by bee men from all parts of the country.

The funeral will be held on Wednesday afternoon from the home at 2 o'clock. Burial in Elmlawn cemetery."

Five years later:

1930 Friedemann Greiner's only son, Harold Greiner was struck and killed by a car –

May 1930, *Democrat and Chronicle,* Rochester, NY

"Harold J Greiner of Macedon, formerly of Naples, was instantly killed Sunday about midnight on May 18, 1930, in an automobile accident on the Fairport-Palmyra Road. Mr. Greiner, who conducted a garage at Macedon, had been called by Wilson Fisher, also of Macedon, to tow his car, which had developed motor trouble. As Mr. Greiner reached the scene, one of the tires on his service car blew out. While he was changing the tire, Fisher saw a large sedan coming directly toward them and shouted to Mr. Greiner, but before he could escape the sedan struck him.

The driver of the sedan and his companions abandoned their car and fled from the scene. Authorities later arrested Anthony Spagnolia, 17, of Rochester, on a charge of manslaughter and held him without bail. It is claimed that Spagnolia, injured and bloodstained, sought and obtained a ride from Macedon to his home in Rochester, and that later the one who had given him the "lift" led the authorities to Spagnolia's home, where he was found. The car which he was driving was said to have been a stolen one, and it is also claimed that he had stolen another car a few hours earlier and that he had had another accident preceding the one resulting in Mr. Greiner's death.

Harold J. Greiner was the son of Friedemann and Bertha Jennings Greiner and was born in Naples on November 30, 1899, and most of his life was passed in this town. He was a graduate of Naples High School and Teachers' Training Class, and had taught school for a few years. Upon the death of his father, Harold took over the extensive Greiner apiary near this village, which he conducted until about two years ago, when he removed to Macedon and engaged in the garage business. For several years he had been secretary of the New York State Beekeepers' Association. He was a member of the Naples Methodist Church, and of John Hodge Lodge No. 815, F. and A. M., of this village, and of Naples Grange. Mr. Greiner was united in marriage at Saratoga Springs with Miss Harriet Wells, of Gloversville, who survives. Other survivors include two small children, Harold Frederick and Catherine, of Macedon; his mother, Mrs. Bertha J. Greiner, of Macedon, and two sisters, Mrs. Sophia Olney, of Macedon, and Mrs. H. E. Shaw, of Buffalo. Funeral services will be held from the Methodist church in this village this afternoon at 2:30 o'clock, conducted by the pastor, Rev. William Partington, and interment will be made in Rose Ridge cemetery. John Hodge Lodge, F. and A. M., will have charge of the services at the grave.

TUISCO GREINER

The death of Mr. Greiner makes at least eight tragic deaths in the Greiner family within the past two generations. His father, Friedemann Greiner, was killed by the accidental discharge of a shotgun which he was carrying in a truck while driving along the Hunts Hollow Road in 1922. Guthart (sic) Greiner, a brother of Friedemann, died as the result of an automobile accident at Niagara Falls, and Paul Greiner, a son (nephew) of Guthart, was killed when struck by the limb of a tree while working in the woods in Garlinghouse. Another Paul Greiner, brother of Albin Greiner, now of Naples, and a son of the late Tuisco Greiner, brother of Friedemann and Guthart (sic), was killed by a train at LaSalle. About 18 years ago Carl Goodrich, son of Mortimer and Carrie Greiner Goodrich, was drowned in Niagara River (Lake Erie); Mrs. Goodrich was a sister (niece) of Friedemann, (Carrie was the daughter of Gotthold), Guthart (sic) and Tuisco. Harold Griener (sic), as above stated, was killed by an automobile Sunday night. At least two other members of the family met tragic deaths in Germany."

It's not clear what other two tragedies in Germany the writer here was referring to. I was able to find a few that might qualify:

Brother Ludwig wrote:

"Uncle Leo b. Dec 28, 1812 - disappeared in 1839. He was a painter, too. We owned one of his pictures until a short time ago. Father had a uniform cap from him which is all eaten up by moths now, but we have a briefcase which he bought in Belgium. It had many notes and drawings (in) it. He seemed to be homesick and must have missed his mother. He must have moved there in 1832. From there he went to France and as Legionaire (sic) to Algier. (sic)"

Florine died at 30 years of age on May 1, 1838 in Friederichsanfang. She is said to have been shot by a former lover.

Brother August Ludwig Greiner said she was a "stepsister" of his grandfather, Ernst Friederich Ferdinand Greiner, while one family tree on ancestry.com said she was a Foster daughter.

Yet another tragedy had occurred in the Greiner family - some years before that. According to the "*glashuttenprivileg*", (glass hut privilege) of 1486, glasshut, or glass factory owners, having a larger workforce, had the right, or privilege, to build their own breweries. In those days, beer was heartier and considered more as a nourishing food, than an alcoholic drink. It also helped to keep the men hydrated while working so closely to the extreme heat of the ovens as they were shaping the molten glass.

About 300 years later, the Greiner brewery would inadvertently play a role in Gotthelf Greiner's future. He would become the great-grandfather of the three immigrant brothers that settled in Garlinghouse.

In his memoirs, Gotthelf wrote of his brother:

"My father tried to persuade me to study, because regardless of this I have a younger brother, who will one day assume the rights to the glass factory, and I as the oldest must leave Limbach.... My father and tutor were certainly right that I still had a younger brother, but the wise providence of God had chosen me and held me back to provide for my parents' livelihood as a glassmaker, as seen in the following sequence. My youngest brother was killed in a vat of hot beer, so I now found myself compelled to take over the glassworks business because I had no further brothers. My mother gave birth to several children (13), but they died early in their tender childhood."

Later in Gotthelf's memoirs, he mentions his brother's death again:

"My youngest brother was killed by falling into a vat of hot beer in the brewing house and died 12 hours later. My father was not home at the time, and then when he came home he was already buried. This needs no further description; anyone with feelings, would applaud me (literally translated), that my father was completely penetrated by this loss and his pain, that he did not know what to do or where to start from all of his grief. He began drinking brandy to drive away his depression, and thus his wealth too, was steadily disappearing. He was also incapable of doing anything of use in the household."

Go ahead, take a break, dry your eyes and sigh a deep, refreshing sigh - I promise the rest of the book will not be so bad.

In the meantime, the next section will certainly cheer you up…

I promise!

Chapter Eleven

Life Is What You Make of It

"…for gardening, like life, is what you make of it – a paradise of pleasure or a veritable sheol of drudgery."

Introduction T. Greiner, Autumn 1894
How to Make the Garden Pay

The Summer House

Fig. 5. A summer house.

The Garden Book for Practical Farmers
by Tuisco Greiner

The Garden House and Old Glory

I have to admit, it's impossible for me *not* to dwell on the following paragraphs. Tuisco's description of his summer garden house leaves me with a dreamy longing to be there – an irresistible expectation that I can simply jump in my car and drive the 106 miles or so to great Grandpa's house in La Salle, to sit with him there in the vine covered garden house just as he describes it below…

"I can not (sic) forbear to say, however, that my daily visits to, and my daily work in, the garden during the entire summer season are my chief pleasures. The sun seems to be too tardy in the morning for my impatience to take my accustomed trip through the various patches and to observe what progress each crop or plant has made during the night; and darkness comes far too soon in the evening for my anxiety to remain longer in company of my plant pets."

"A great country this is-a country of thrift, of energy, of feverish activity! Yet often in our mad rush for the accumulation of the means that would enable us to live a life of ease and comfort, we forget to enjoy the comforts that we have within easy reach. I believe that the far poorer opportunities and vastly inferior privileges, average well-to-do Old Country people are taking life far easier, and enjoy more of life's blessings and comforts than many of us do here.

Many a pleasant hour have I spent in friendly chats with acquaintances, or in profitable meditation or study, in the little summer house in our own garden at home, or in that of neighbors. Comparatively few are the gardens in the country where I first saw the light of day, without a summer house of some kind. Usually it is a cheap, simple frame or lattice work, round, square or octagonal, and a roof of the same material, vine-surrounded, vine roofed. There is a plain table in the center, plain wooden benches or rustic chairs at the sides. Here you may rest in peace. The busy hum of insects, the merry twitter of birds, the fragrances of flowers will lull you into drowsy forgetfulness or earthly ills. And if you desire more substantial blessings than these, stretch forth your hand and gather the luscious clusters of grapes that are suspended within your reach through the lattice work of the roof and sides."

"Or step forth from the house to the bed beyond, and tickle your palate with the spicy strawberry, or the fragrant raspberry, or whatever fruit the season may offer.

Is there any earthly reason why American farmers should not have summer houses, and enjoy all these privileges held out to them so lavishly by nature's hand?"

The Garden Book for Practical Farmers (1901) Pgs. 27-32

"Of Thee I Sing"

"I care not what country was the land of my forefathers. This Union of States with its vast opportunities, the productiveness of its farms and gardens, and the wonderful generosity of its climate, is the land of my choice-the grandest country on earth.

Would you live in God's grandest garden county, yet be "the man without the garden?" There is a class of men that can do this very thing. They are not the ones for whom this book is written.... They might set down right in the middle of the Garden of Eden, yet they would see nothing but the drudgery of hell. Worse than that. They would bring up their children in complete ignorance of all the beauties surrounding them, and just keep them tied down to the task of digging around the apple trees all day."

The Garden Book for Practical Farmers (1901) Pg. 34

A Taste for Finer Things....

"Here is for instance a little story told on good authority of that human nightingale, Mlle. Calvé, whose sweet notes and trills I had the good fortune to listen to on several occasions with unbounded delight:

"'Mlle. Calve is probably the only great prima donna who combines farming with her brilliant operatic achievements. She has a large farm at Cevennes and rusticates there each Summer. Last summer the famous singer went into her own kitchen garden and cared for her own vegetables. No one was allowed to touch them, and the results were far better than when her gardener cared for things. Mlle. Calve wore a short skirt of blue jeans, sabots and a linen shirt waist. She spaded and hoed and watered her vegetables day after day, and proudly sent gifts of the finest fruits of her labors to friends in Paris.

The prima donna was very ill and nervous when she went to Cevennes, but this free open air life and the vigorous exercise soon restored her to the most robust health, and when friends asked her the secret of her cure she answered: 'Spades and potatoes.'"

>The Garden Book For Practical Farmers (1896) Pgs. 13

…Yet Champion of the Common Man.

"How amusing to see some of these city clerks in city or village stores strutting about with an air of superiority – all for $8 or $10 a week. And how condescendingly, from their exalted station, they treat their lowly farmer customer.

Yet this same lowly farmer must be a pretty well-informed salesman himself, if he wants to secure the best returns from his wares…. He also has to be a very thorough sort of book-keeper… machinist, chemist, pathologist, entomologist, veterinarian, carpenter and often a blacksmith."

>The Garden Book For Practical Farmers (1896) Pgs. 16

Life Is What You Make of It

"…You have the decision in your hands. You may leisurely accompany your visitors through the well-kept grounds that are beaming with thrifty, sparkling vegetation, as your own countenance is beaming with pleasure and satisfaction and that is as free from weeds as your face is from care; or you may crawl through the beds on hands and knees, piling up stacks of weeds, with a face sour and distorted in hatred of yourself and the life you are leading...."

Introduction T. Greiner, Autumn 1894
How to Make the Garden Pay

Chapter Twelve

For Love of the Garden

<u>The Man With The Garden</u>
If I could put my words in song,
And tell what's there enjoyed,
All men would to my garden throng,
And leave the cities void

Ralph Waldo Emerson

Tuisco's Farm ca 1901

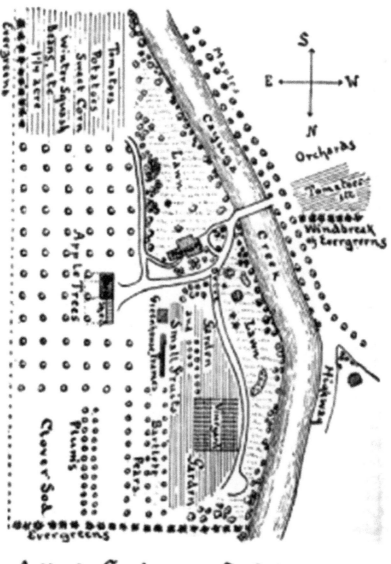

pg. 64 – The Garden Book for Practical Farmers Vol. I
by Tuisco Greiner

TUISCO GREINER

1908 Map of "E. A. Long" Property
La Salle, Niagara, NY

This map has been oriented South to North as Tuisco's drawing was. (aka "turned upside down")

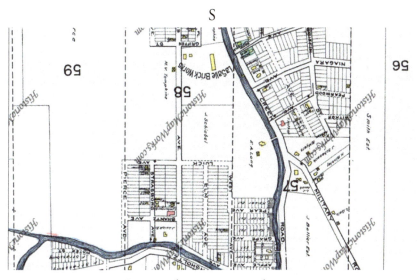

Courtesy historicmapworks.com

Tuisco lived on the E.A. Long farm at the time this map was made. Pearwood Ave. would later become Lindburgh Ave., which was extended east, across Creek Road, through the Lawn area south of the house. Brother Gotthold lived close by, with his daughter Carrie Goodrich and her family - also on Pearwood Ave., but on the west side of Cayuga Creek.

"After all that has been said in the preceding chapter, the reader will not wonder that I place agriculture in the foremost rank among all the different occupations of mankind; that I can not think of a more exalted station in life's works than that of the soil tiller."

Chapter II - The Garden Book For Practical Farmers - 1896

"Times and conditions have changed. The land does not respond any more quite so promptly to merely scratching its back with plow and harrow. It has grown weary and hungry. It now looks for food, and coaxing and petting, before it can be made to smile with flowers, fruits, vegetables and grains."

Practical Farm Chemistry–Introduction
Copyrighted 1891 by T. Greiner, La Salle, N.Y.

"The condition of many a home garden seems sufficient cause for hiding it from sight… A good garden is a sort of summer resort, to which the owner can take his visitors, and show them about with excusable pride; an inducement for an after-dinner, or after-supper walk… nearness to the house means nearness to your thoughts and affections…"

How to Make The Garden Pay 1890 - Pg. 19

In response to a reader's question regarding the use of stable manure on the garden:
"It may be necessary to make annual application of stable manure to secure best results in garden crops, but it has always seemed like shooting sparrows with cannonballs."

The Rural New Yorker, June 30, 1906

Chapter Thirteen

An Opinionated Man

"I cannot suppress a friendly suggestion…"

Tuisco Greiner - "Fireside and Hearth" 1891

"I may justly be proud of the enemies I have made."

Tuisco Greiner

March 11, 1908 – *Niagara Falls Gazette*

"Brother Tuisco went to a seminar but had to leave because of his free thinking religious direction which didn't harmonize with one of the managers. Then he worked for the Post Office but couldn't keep the job because he couldn't keep things to himself"

August Ludwig Greiner

I believe God blesses each of his creations with a purpose in life complete with strengths and talents unique to each person. Some of us are born to tell "it" like it is – and some of us have to spend a lifetime being "tested by fire" before we learn for sure, what "it" is.

"Schwabenhans Greiner prided himself on being a descendant of Graf Eberhardt der Greiner" (Count Eberhardt the Cantankerous)

This comment was found on a family tree online, and quoted by other Greiner cousins. I was unable to find a source, but I've heard several Greiners admit to having a Cantankerous Greiner streak in themselves. Some have even gone so far as to suggest that I might have a bit of that in me - and judging by the hearty way Grandma brushed my hair, when I was 5, (while mumbling something about rat's nests), I would say she did, too.

The name Greiner, is translated to mean "cantankerous, quarreler, squabbler" – (ancestry.com.) Literally like an irritating grain of sand.

If "Count Eberhardt the Cantankerous" is indeed Tuisco's ancestor, then, Tuisco has certainly lived up to the name - although, his opinions sound, to me, more like good advice – with a slight lean toward cantankerous. I'm sure his fellow politicians felt the irritation of quite of few grainy sands more than his agricultural readers did… and so they should!

March 9, 1882 - *The Neapolitan*

"…. It seems to me that the people of this town should appreciate the privilege of buying first-class seeds right at home! There are not many towns the size of Naples, where it can be done! Now will you go and buy second-class or stale seeds such as are left to be sold on commission at the stores? I expect you will patronize me. Let each store sell its kind. The seed trade should belong to me! …"

"…. My remarks may prove to be helpful to them, and offered as suggestions rather than criticisms…. the most interesting and valuable of all station bulletins, and it would seem ungrateful to offer criticisms. Still I cannot suppress a friendly suggestion… In fact some of these newspaper bulletins are edited so carelessly that they are utterly worthless."

Tuisco Greiner in "Fireside and Hearth" 1891

SOME SUGGESTIONS FOR OUR EXPERIMENT STATIONS
By Joseph (aka Tuisco) Greiner

Article Excerpts:

"I am not a habitual fault-finder, I hope. Especially do I dislike to find fault with the agricultural experiment stations. Some of them do admirable work, and are a great help to farmers and farming interests generally…"

"…Some of these publications are absolutely and utterly worthless without any practical points and without usefulness to the practical farmer, and most of them are edited in an abominable manner. Often, we cannot make head or tail to it. In many of these bulletins I am unable to find a single point worth mentioning or commenting on in the rural press. Precious few of them are even readable…."

"The man who willfully and needlessly deprives his family of the privileges of a good vegetable garden fails in one of his foremost duties. He cannot possibly be a good husband, nor a good father, *and he certainly is not a good Christian!*"

"How To Make The Garden Pay" 1890

(Italics and exclamation are Tuisco's)

Nov. 19, 1890 - *Chautauqua News*

"You Can Obtain HASH almost anywhere, but if you want Simon-pure ORIGINAL Matter by **such celebrated writers** as T. B., Terry, John Gould, Henry Stewart, B.F. Johnson, Waldo P. Brown, Wm. Falconer, Galen Wilson, **T. Greiner**, John M. Stahl and a score or more of the **best common-sense writers in the country**, you must subscribe for The Practical Farmer

Pronounced the Best 16-Page Agricultural Weekly in America. It will be sent every week from now to Jan. 1, '92, for One Dollar. Sample Copies Free to All"

(dictionary.com: to hash over; to bring up again for consideration; discuss, especially in review.)

September 3, 1902 - *The Arcadian Weekly Gazette*

T. Greiner of La Salle, Niagara county, writes Interesting fruit letters to the Tribune Farmer. Of the apple crop, he speaks as follows in the last Issue:

"The city dailies have recently brought glowing accounts, written up by special reporters, of our wonderful crop of late apples. I don't see where that crop is. I have seen no large crops anywhere in this county, nor in any other county of Western New York which I have happened to pass through. My Impression is that apples will not be plentiful this fall, and really good or fancy ones will be quite scarce. We find few trees with good foliage. The apple scab is prevalent everywhere, apparently even where trees have been repeatedly sprayed. Two years ago, I had a full crop of late apples, which I sold at $1.50 to $ 3 per barrel. This year I have not more than a quarter or a third of that crop, and the individual apples are much poorer in appearance.

This is in line with what conservative observers in this town have seen. When dealers tell you that the apple crop is immense and that the prices will be low, make allowances. You have heard the same story every year. Certainly, since the apple scab developed, the prospects are poor for first class barrelled stock, consequently prices will be good later, if not at first. Evaporated stock and cider stock will be more plenty, but not to the extent of making prices exceedingly low. Newark evaporators are offering only 85 cents a hundred, but we notice by Rochester papers that in other towns they are paying from 15 to 25 cents a bushel. Don't be in a hurry to sell your apple crop."

TUISCO GREINER

August 18, 1906 - *The Rural New Yorker*

"T. Greiner writes:

'Bloomless, seedless, worthless—this fits any of the kind of apple trees which I recently located in various parts of the country. In Virginia, West Virginia, Ohio, etc. and for which nobody that can get a good apple has any particular use. There are too many in the country to concede to them much value even as a curiosity.'"

November 4, 1907 – *Niagara Gazette*

"DUDLEY'S PAPER GIVES STRANGE ADVICE TO PEOPLE OF LA SALLE Circular Knocking Mr. Dudley's Lighting Service Was Folded in Copies Of the Niagara Falls News.

The people of the village of La Salle, or rather that portion of the population who subscribe to the Niagara Falls News, are mystified over a circular that came to them on Saturday evening folded in the copies of that paper.

The circular was in the nature of an open letter to the people of the village of La Salle, and it had to do with the lighting situation there as well as with other matters. It was signed by Tusico Greiner, president of the village.

Now, as is well known, there has been a great deal of complaint against the electric light service afforded that village by the company of which Frank A. Dudley of this city is at the head, and to find such a circular included within the folds of Mr. Dudley's newspaper was certainly a great surprise to the people of the village.

This same circular letter appeared in the columns of the Cataract-Journal several days ago, and in view of the interests involved, It was hardly expected that the News would take it up and scatter it among Mr. Dudley's patrons. Doubtless an explanation is due from some source... La Salle, N. Y., Nov. 1, 1907."

T. GREINER, Village Pres.

March 11, 1908 – *Niagara Falls Gazette*
LETTERS TO THE EDITOR
La Salle, N. Y.-March 11, 1908.
Editor Niagara Falls Gazette: Niagara Falls, New York.

"Dear Sir: Believing that it is not the settled policy of the GAZETTE to willfully and maliciously point misstatements or contortions of facts, I may have the privilege to state to you and to your readers that my friends in both parties, had right along been given to understand that I was not going to allow my name to be considered for renomination as president of the village.

Everyone at all familiar with the conditions in this community knows that I have today as many as firm friends in the village of La Salle and in the Town of Niagara as I ever had. I have no opposition whatever in the better elements of both parties, and I may justly be proud of the enemies I have made."

Yours Respectfully,

T. GREINER

I almost felt sorry for Tuisco because of the many nay-sayers, as well as the insults and ridicule he suffered… now I know how he really felt. He didn't seem to suffer much from self-pity, did he? Why should he, really? Whatever he did, he did it with a passion that might have offended some, but he did it, not just to further his career, but to do what was fair and right and helpful for the people he served – in his writing, and as a public servant.

(On the other hand, I suspect his family might have had a hard time living under the same roof with him.)

A defense of justice – with a tiny glimpse of Tuisco's boyhood, and a touch of sarcastic wit:

July 7, 1908 – *Niagara Falls Gazette*
THE SCHOOL QUESTION AGAIN

"Editor Gazette: Dear Sir: ' If it be true (as you allege in your editorial July 3rd, using a rather cheap argument) that I do not have a full insight in the compulsory education law, it can not be blamed on my lack of opportunity to study and its workings. For more than a dozen years of my boyhood I have attended school under the then Justly famous compulsory education system of Germany. For an almost equal length of time, more recently, I have, as trustee, been in closest touch with the school masters in our own district, a graded school, and both as trustee and justice, I have done what probably very few trustees or other local school boards and very few Justices have done, namely at the sacrifice of much time and effort, have personally investigated every one of the many cases of alleged violations of the school law that were brought before me...."

"If after having had all these opportunities, I am as well informed about the workings of this school law as I might, it would have to be assumed that nature has denied me that gift of discernment, of powers of observation and logical reasoning which Mr. Sullivan in his office in Albany, Mr. Cary in his law office, or you in your editorial sanctum must possess in a so much higher degree in order to be able to arrive at correct conclusions without any knowledge whatever of the underlying facts and to judge without evidence...

Perhaps you know that the holdup of the one-half of your public money was an afterthought of Mr. Sullivan's, apparently inspired by the attitude taken by your own Board of Education; and I predict that the Commissioner of Education will pay over every cent of that money just as soon as the bluff is called.

To go over the school question in all its various ramifications, to show where the Commissioner of Education is overreaching, and doing incalculable harm thereby, and to present all the details of the evidence I have in my possession in support of my allegations, would require the space of many pages of the GAZETTE.

All the squabbles with your local court, the person or personalities of the judge or his political leanings, are all matters of minor importance. The great question is how to meet most effectively the attempts of the Commissioner to usurp powers and functions that are not in his province, and how to maintain at least a remnant of local self government—and your own self respect. It is up to the city, up to its Board of Education. Call the bluff, Mr. Cary."

La Salle, N. Y, July 6, 1908.

T. GREINER

One more opinion piece, gives us an ironic little vignette into the history of our beloved "Wine Country" of the Finger Lakes:

TEMPERANCE

PROHIBITION PROHIBIT? SOME "FACTS" FROM OUR GOOD FRIEND T. GREINER.

"How absurd, and how easily disproved by the facts, is this claim of the liquor men that prohibition does not prohibit: how, just at this time, by denials and misstatements and misrepresentations, they try to wiggle out of the hole that the unexampled and wonderful prosperity of the dry State of Kansas has put them in! And this prosperity cannot be denied. Our good friend F.D. Coburn vouches for it as against the whole of the liquor forces.

We have in New York one county that is wholly dry. This is Yates. It has one large village, Penn Yan, which has been dry for over four years. I was anxious to learn how things look there now, and asked Assemblyman Gillette some pointed questions. The following are the facts as reported to me:

During the year of *license*, 210 persons were arrested in Penn Yan, 118 of them for intoxication. During the four years of *no license* (Oct. 1, 1909, to same date 1913), the number of arrests was gradually reduced to 96, 91, 81, and 90, respectively, of which numbers 74, 55, 62, and 53, respectively were for intoxication. In the slightly larger village of Canandaigua, a license town with the large brewery in Ontario County, probably not more than 20 miles distant, 710 persons, 411 of them for intoxication, were arrested during the year 1912. Some difference, apparently!

It is true that some liquor has been brought and shipped into Penn Yan during the dry years, and that there have been cases of intoxication. But it is also true that no divine commandment, no law made by man, has had the effect of entirely stopping the prohibited practice or acts. Our state laws prohibit murder and assault and larceny, etc.: but murdering and assaulting and stealing are going on just the same. What sane person would think of repealing our criminal laws for that reason?

Penn Yan is the county-seat of Yates Co. Since it voted dry, there has been so little business for the police court there that the people voted to abolish the office of police justice, a salary of $600 per year, for the apparent reason that the justices of the peace are fully able to take care of the reduced number of criminal cases. Moreover, when county court was called on June 9, 1913, there was not a single case, either civil or criminal to be tried. It was a surprising and wholly unprecedented situation.

"It may be a coincidence," says one commentator, "but it is a most gratifying fact that this unheard-of condition occurred while Yates Co. did not have a legalized bar within its borders." It is no wonder, then, that the great majority of Penn Yan's physicians, eleven in number, ask the voters of Milo Township to vote "No" on all four propositions, and that every grange in Yates Co. has passed resolutions in favor of no license."

HOW PROHIBITION AFFECTS THE BANKS.

The two banks in Penn Yan report the following amounts of deposit:

Report of Sept. 14, 1909, the last during *license*.

Total	$928,382.00
Nov. 16, 1909, first during *no license*	1,106.811.00
Nov. 10, 1910, *no license*	1,151,440.04
Dec. 21, 1911, *no license*	1,158,439.41

A total increase under the no-license years of $400,280.53

No wonder the banks and their depositors are in favor of *no license!*

Finally let me quote the substance of Assemblyman Gillette's personal reply to my questions:

"As to conditions here, they certainly are better than they were when liquor was openly sold. A great deal of liquor is brought here and slyly sold. But we seldom see a drunken man on the street. Almost without exception the merchants are in favor of the dry town now. I think that every place which used to be used for a saloon is now occupied by some legitimate business, but some of them at far lower rents. The owners of property which was used as saloons, and the hotels, have been hit pretty hard; but all other kinds of business are well satisfied. Factories and all employers of labor like it much better, as their men are sober and ready to go to work Monday morning.

What have the liquor men to say to such facts and statements? Will they claim that "prohibition does not prohibit?"

T. Greiner. La Salle, N.Y., July 24.
- Gleanings Bee Culture Vol. 42, pg 656

And finally, some would return the favor....

March 2, 1903 - *Lockport Journal*
PEACH KING'S SPEECH
Hon. J. H. Hale Speaks Before the Farmers' Club
Gas at Gasport.
BRIGHTEST HIT IN ITS HISTORY.

"Mr. Hale Addresses a Crowded House at Gasport on Saturday—Many Lock port (sic) Citizens Present—How the Greatest Peach Business in the World was Built Up.

...During this time Mr. Hale had been answering questions, and was admonished by President Hopkins that it would be better to reserve the answers until after the slides had all been shown, as the supply of gas was short. "What," said the Connecticut "peach," "short of gas in Gasport, impossible." To a previous inquirer who addressed him as "Govenor," he remarked testily, "Don't call me governor." In a previous speech, Tuisco Greiner had taken issue with the "Governor." He paid for it by sustaining a running fire of good natured raillery all through the two hours address, which highly amused the audience...."

Older and Wiser - Self-Assessment

"I myself have perhaps been a more severe critic of my own work than the great mass of my readers who have been so universally and often undeservedly kind to me and my efforts. I could not blind my own eyes to the fact, however, that serious shortcomings did exist ..."

T. Greiner Autumn 1894 - How to Make the Garden Pay

"The older I grow, the less I am inclined to feel 'cock-sure' about anything."

The Rural New Yorker, June 30, 1906

Chapter Fourteen

Benefits of a Proper Diet

"The American people are getting to be more and more weaned from the flesh-pots of old Yankeedom, and into the habit of substituting therefor the fruits of the promised land. This means a steady move in the right direction – away from an excessive and almost exclusive meat diet, and toward civilization and refinement."

Tuisco Greiner Celery for Profit 1893 – Pg. 10

Antique Seed Packet

Courtesy Clearly Vintage Blogspot

"...one of the choicest, most palatable, and most wholesome vegetables that were ever brought under cultivation....

Much might also be said about the sanitary, if not the medical effects of a celery diet. This vegetable is generally recognized as a nerve tonic and nerve stimulant. Its free use makes you stronger, healthier, and it may save you doctors' visits and outlays for medicines. If it saves expense, it has a money value, and is profitable. And then, health is worth more than money."

"Celery for Profit" -pgs. 11, 13

And if that description of celery sounds overstated, try an online search for "health benefits of celery".

It seems that it: boosts the immune system, promotes a healthy heart, regulates blood sugar/diabetes, lowers blood pressure, prevents cancer and other diseases, relieves stress, eases joint pain, delays vision loss due to aging, lowers bad cholesterol, detoxifies the body, balances acidity, has anti-inflammatory properties, diuretic . . . and a long list of other benefits—including one claim that it has pheromones that improve your love life!

Tuisco's wise advice in the following excerpts, is very convincing:

Proper Diet

"The stomach, therefore is the pivotal point around which all the rest revolves. Put proper food into a normal stomach and the result will be good blood, and consequently mental, physical and moral health."

Builds Character

"...the food, the stomach, the blood, play an important part in determining character of the human being, and his usefulness (or otherwise)..."

A Tried and True Drugstore

"Now in what relation does the garden stand to all this? I maintain, and will attempt to prove, that it furnishes… safer cathartics, better kidney and nerve stimulants, and other medicines of greater efficiency than any we find on the shelves of our regulation drug stores."

"No drugstore in the world has a nicer, safer, and more resultful assortment of medicines for the various ills that mankind is heir to than is found in nature's laboratory in the vegetable and fruit garden. For the truth of this proposition is not wanting".

Cure For Spring Fever

"What are these "spring fevers" and tired feelings of which so many country people complain of at the close of winter? Nothing but the effects of winter's injudicious feeding. The feverish condition disappears with the return to a diet in which fruits, vegetables, eggs, milk, fish, chickens, etc., form a more prominent part."

"An apple a day
Sends the doctor away,"

is an old popular saying. Who would expect to cure a disease of long standing with one or two doses of medicine? We are not looking for wonders. Strawberries are a mild, safe and most pleasant physic. So is pie-plant or rhubarb. So are onions and carrots. Asparagus, dandelions, spinach, etc., stimulate liver and kidney action. We don't expect that a single plate of strawberries, a mess of asparagus or spinach, will have much or lasting effect. It is the continued use of these materials in our ration which tells.

A good physician gives you a bottle of medicine compounded of more or less harmless, and perhaps even ineffective, materials. You are to take a small quantity two or three times a day. Then he gives you explicit directions about your diet, what to eat and what to abstain from during the whole course of treatment. The treatment is long continued. You expect the medicine is curing you. The physician knows better; he has simply tried to balance your ration to rest your stomach and digestive powers, and let nature do the rest… in short, both with animals and human beings, we must look to the food supply, and use what nature intended for our use and food, in order to maintain normal conditions, health and happiness."

The Lemon Cure

"I am convinced that typhoid-fever germs lurk in many wells, and for that reason have become afraid of well water as a beverage, pure as it may appear and good as it may be to the taste, unless either boiled or medicated. The medication has usually consisted of the addition of plenty of lemon juice. Lemon juice is likewise known to destroy the germs of diphtheria, and undoubtedly other infectious disease."

Cure for Alcoholism

"The uncontrollable craving for alcoholic drinks is not a natural condition; it is a disease. Its primary cause is improper nutrition. It is not so much the saloon which makes drunkards, although it helps a bad cause along."

"The kitchen of the people without the garden is the place where many cases of drink habit are started;

Parents may set to their children a good example of temperate habits; they may send them to good schools, to church and to temperance lectures, and will try to keep them away from saloons and from all temptation. But as long as from ignorance or shiftlessness they fail to supply their children's bodies with the proper food in well-balanced ration, refuse to them a reasonable quantity of succulent vegetables and acid fruits, and to neglect to instill into them the main principles of hygienic living which forbid excesses in eating as well as in drinking, they must primarily and chiefly held responsible if such gross mistakes result in blood clogged with impurities – morbid cravings and finally in overindulgence of alcoholic drinks. The responsibility can not all be unloaded upon the bad company and the salon. Most people may be fed in such a way that they will not seek a cure for bodily ills in the cup that inebriates."

Beautiful Skin

"Furthermore, it can hardly be doubted that a vegetable is the best of all cosmetics. What Dr. J. H. Kellogg says in Good Health about the use of fruits for the purpose of insuring a clear skin, may well be applied with equal justification to the use of succulent vegetables."

"The following is a quotation:"

'A preparation of apples, grapes, cherries, figs, bananas and other kinds of fruits, combined with nuts of various kinds – almonds, pecans, hickory nuts – and with well-cooked grains, applied to the inside of the stomach, is the best possible preparation for whitening the skin. The trouble with the skin when it is dingy and dirty is that the dirt is more than skin deep. There are also dirty muscles and a dirty brain, dirty glands, dirty blood; the whole body is contaminated; the dingy color of the skin is merely a sign of the condition of the whole body. Simply to bleach the dirt off the face is a very hypocritical procedure. We may make the skin of the face clean while the rest of the body is filled with organic dirt, tissue debris and effete, worn out and diseased matter which has accumulated as the result of vital work and improper diet. We should be interested in the whole skin rather than in the skin of the face alone. To be beautiful we must eat beautiful things. What beautiful cheek a ripe peach has! Who could wish a complexion more beautiful than the bloom of a peach? The way to get such a bloom is to use the peach itself.'

(Kellogg)

"In short, the powerful combination of "dirt, disease and the devil" (to use the words of a famous preacher) can best be fought by means of perfect nutrition."

A Man's Responsibility to His Family

"Can you, as a man, husband, as father, afford to be the man without the garden – without a garden that furnishes these needed foods, the vegetables and small fruits which put pure blood into the bodies of those dearest to you, the bloom of the rose into their cheeks, which keeps their minds clear, their morals untarnished, and wards off the dreaded attacks of infectious diseases? …. its services are far greater and more potent than that of the doctor and the druggist. In most cases you could safely discharge them both, and rely on nature's doctoring and dispensation of drugs. And the garden charges you no doctor's fees nor druggist profits."

The Garden Book for Practical Farmers (1901) - Pgs. 20-32

Chapter Fifteen

The "Ingenious" Greiner Brothers

"…. their saws run as near perfect as mechanical skill can make them. They have rigged them on purpose for their business, and are now busily at Work manufacturing their three hundred hives…"

April 1, 1876 - Naples Record

The Greiner Brothers

Contributed by Jose Greiner, Grandson of Tuisco & Cora Greiner
L-R: Gotthold, Tuisco, Friedemann

The Greiner Brothers wasted no time in branching out from farming to a variety of business adventures:

Building Sleighs

January 22, 1876 - *The Naples Record*

"The Greiner Brothers at the head of Hunts Hollow have made and have on hand two new, well made and finished sleighs; they warrant the wood work and ironing to be of the best; they wish to sell them at reasonable prices. They can be seen at their residence near French's and all who want will be satisfied when they examine them. They give notice that they will make to order and repair anything in the sleigh; line and warrant their work. Call on them."

At the Fair

Oct. 9, 1876 - *Ontario Repository and Messenger*

"Glass boxes of honey of the purest white, ornamented with gilded borders, by the Greiner Bros., made a nice, and tempting display, and the Union Bee Hive, also on exhibition, seemed to possess many advantages above the common hive."

October 1, 1880 - *Geneva Gazette*

The following premiums were awarded at the Union Fair of the Pre-emption Park limited, Geneva, held Sept. 21,22, 23,1880:

Best sample honey, Greiner Bros, Naples... 1.00

Manufacturing Bee Hives

January 22, 1876 - *The Naples Record*

"F.H. Frink and G.C. Greiner both of this town have secured the right to manufacture and sell the celebrated Alverson Union Bee Hive and will supply the town the coming season. Greiner Brothers will do all the transferring from any old hive to the above named hive as soon as the season will admit, for all who may call on them."

February 5, 1876 - *The Naples Record*

"F.H. Frink has sold out his interest in the Union Bee Hive to Greiner Brothers, who will now attend to all who want. "G. G. Greiner" has been out a couple of days and took orders for fifty hives ___ so ___ is the rush for them. It is a fine _____ and every bee grower needs just as many as he has swarms."

April 1, 1876 - *The Naples Record*

"—Greiner Bros, started their machinery last Wednesday; everything works complete, and their saws run as near perfect as mechanical skill can make them. They have rigged them on purpose for their business, and are now busily at Work manufacturing their three hundred hives, which they agreed to furnish this spring. They say they can not canvass any more, as it will take all their time to get ready for spring business. If any wish to try their hives and have any transferring done by them, that have not, already given their orders, they must do so soon! They are also prepared to do work in workmanlike manner, and furnish anything connected with their hive, and will keep on hand Kidd's frame, boxes, tights and all the fixings belonging to the hive."

January 1, 1877 - *The Naples Record*

"—We learn that Greiner Bros, have secured the agency of Yates County. for the Alverson's Union Hive. We congratulate the citizens of our neighboring county that they are to have an opportunity to use this best of hives yet invented! Its good qualities are only to be seen and they will be readily recognized. We never have heard of a farmer who was sorry he changed.

—The Union Beehive has pleased the bee growers so well that the Greiner Bros. are making arrangements to manufacture a larger number than ever next spring. "G. H. Greiner" will canvass this vicinity for the spring work, and those who wish to make bee-keeping pay better should patronize this hive"

May 5, 1877 - *The Naples Record*

"—Greiner Bros, are preparing for a good spring's job; with last spring's experience to work on, they are manufacturing better hives, and will give satisfaction in every respect.

—We would say to those who use the Union Hive, and do not wish to see to themselves, that we are prepared to do it for them through the season at reasonable charges; we will also prevent swarming if required. GREINER BROS.

—Try the Union Hive; it is no failure and no humbug: we will give in a later issue of The RECORD, a statement of last year's crops which were taken from our hives placed through this town last season. If in some instances the hive has failed to come up to our expectations, it is not the fault of the hive; they are made after one pattern and are perfectly alike. Weak swarms, or perhaps mismanagement was the trouble. GREINER BROS."

May 26, 1877- *Naples Record*

"Greiner Bros, intend to supply all the hives that are wanted for swarming but cannot promise any, unless they are bargained for.

Have your hives ready for swarming; delay in hiving is risky in all cases, and many swarms are lost by being too tardy about it. Greiner Bros, will wait upon you!

We would invite all who are interested in Bee-Keeping to call and see our Bee Yard; we will take pleasure to give any required information in regard to bees or hives, as far as we are able to. GREINER BROS."

April 27, 1878 - *Naples Record*

"Did you see that long spring wagon of Greiner Bros, with their firm name on either side and best of all did you see that load of Union Hives it contained. They are delivering some now, Leave your orders quickly!"

Inventions

August 4, 1877 - *Naples Record*

"The Greiner Brothers are very ingenious. They now have made for themselves a honey extractor that is complete. It consists of a cylinder with revolving frame inside, and into which the new comb is properly placed after the cells are uncapped. The machine produces a swift revolving of the comb and throws the pure honey out; it passes through a tunnel at the bottom into cans and is ready for use free from comb or any foreign matter. These enterprising men are now putting the extracted honey on sale in fruit jars! It is a good way to put it up for all fruit jars are worth all they cost when the honey is gone. Stoddard has the cans for sale."

Honey in Abundance

July 29, 1880 - *Naples Record*

"By the kindness of Mr. Clark we are permitted to copy the following from his returns, which compared with that of 1855—twenty-five years ago—makes an interesting study and shows the increase in Naples in many important respects... This column should be scrap-booked."   ...Greiner Bros, sold 3,500 pounds honey

September 9, 1880 - *Naples Record*

"Greiner Brothers have 3 tons of honey to ship this season. They have hives from which they have taken 400 pounds of surplus honey each."

September 6, 1883 - *Naples Record*

"The comb honey furnished by the Greiner Bros, is very superior this year; they shipped 700 pounds this week."

Aviary Supplies for Sale

October 1877 - *Naples Record*

"Greiner Bros, will sell 15 or 20 swarms of bees! They say they will not sell anything but first class colonies. It pays to buy when you know what you are buying."

July 29, 1881 - *Naples Record*

"We can accommodate with Bees, all who wish to purchase, at the following rates:

Young swarms, without hive, each	$4.00
" " with complete hive	7.00
Old swarms without hive	7.00
" " with complete hive	10.00
New hives without surplus case	2.75
Surplus cases	1.00

Swarms sold by us, are warranted to be ALL RIGHT.
                    GREINER BROS."

Chapter Sixteen

Getting to Know Karl Gotthold Greiner

"Hello! Where is this honey-man?"

Photo taken from his obituary
The Niagara Falls Gazette

Karl Gotthold Greiner
1842 – 1925

Gotthold was the oldest of the Greiner Brothers that came to America. He arrived before the Civil War while the other two came later. While he Registered for the Draft, I was unable to find any record that says he actually served in the war. He's described in some newspaper articles as being "genial".

Civic Duty

<u>Civil War Draft Registration Record</u>
For Livingston. Ontario, Yates, NY
Residence:	July 1, 1863 - Naples, NY
Name:	Gotthold "Goriner"
Age:	21
Occupation:	Farmer
Marital Status:	Unmarried
Place of Birth:	Germany
Remarks:	"Alien, Been here one year"

October 12, 1872 – *Naples Record*

"The annual school meeting at Garlinghouse on Tuesday last, resulted in the election; of S. J. Merrill, Dist. Clerk; G. C, Greiner, Trustee, John Goundry, Collector, and Sidney Merrill, Librarian."

August 15, 1891 - *Naples Record*

"Our annual school meeting resulted in the election of S. J. Merrill for District Clerk; G. C. Greiner, Trustee."

June 10, 1896 - *Naples Record*

"G. C. Greiner is in Canandaigua this week as a juror."

A Farmer & Shepherd

March 30, 1878 - *Naples Record*

"Those garden and flower seeds of G. C. Greiner can be found on sale now When you want. There is no use of talking about any other seeds when you can get his. He warrants them, and those who used his seeds last year will have no other."

February 26, 1890 - *Naples Record*

"G. C. Greiner and brother have purchased three ewes and one ram of a firm in Canada, at the sum of $200. They were received at Bloods on Saturday."

May 28, 1890 – Garlinghouse - *Naples Record*

"Quite an interest had been manifested here among our farmers in sheep husbandry. G.C. Greiner has a flock of very fine thoroughbred Dorsets. They are a very choice grade of sheep and compares well with any others for increase of profitableness. John Goundry takes the lead on choice thoroughbred Shropshires. He has one lamb that at ten weeks of age weighed 74 pounds having gained 25 pounds within the last 21 days. He has several others nearly as heavy. F.H. Frink has also a fine flock of thoroughbred Shropshire."

April 6, 1892 - *Naples Record*

"Last year G.C. Greiner of Garlinghouse grew a large quantity of a new choice variety of early potatoes for a seedsman, and has just shipped them. They go to every state in the union and to Canada. This is a new and remunerative industry, and Mr. Greiner being a most thorough and practical farmer was the first to engage therein."

Active in Church

Before April 15, 1891-*Naples Record*

"Our Sunday school reorganized with the following officers: Superintendant, Perry Bartholomew; Assistant Superintendant, John Goundry; Secretary, S.J. Merrill; Treasurer, Elwin Briggs; Chorister, G.C. Greiner; Organist, Jennie Briggs. We have a large and interesting school, numbering about 15."

At the Fair

September 22, 1881 -*Naples Record*

"Best Honey, G.C. Greiner; second, Caulkins Bros...."

September 10, 1890 -*Naples Record*

Three separate ads:

"Don't Neglect To see the finest sheep in the country—G. C. Greiner's exhibit of Horned Dorsets at the Naples fair next week. No wool and mutton combination is now known. Beyond doubt the Dorset is the coming sheep for North America. Our townsman's flock, though small, is composed of as fine specimens as were ever seen. They have had good pasture since winter, and nothing else. If you want a large, hardy sheep, requiring no extra care, raise the Dorsets."

"I would say that my sheep are not fitted up for fair or exhibition by giving them any extra care whatever. They were turned out to pasture in the early spring and will be taken up the day of the fair. They are well adapted to "rough it.". G. C. GREINER."

"Class No. 5—Horned Dorset, registered. Ram 2 years old— First, G. C. Gremer. Ram 1 year old—First, G. C. Greiner. Ram lamb—First, G. C. Greiner. 8 ewes—First, G. C. Greiner"

September 24, 1890 - *Naples Record*

"The fine show of Shropshire and Dorset sheep by Goundry Bros, and G. C. Greiner elicited much admiration."

October 7, 1891 - *Naples Record*

"Our people speak very highly of the Naples fair and are well pleased with their successes, John Goundry receiving five first and three second premiums on his Shropshire sheep; G. C. Greiner the first on his horned Dorsets; David Wright a first and second on his grade lambs; and Nellis Westbrook a premium on his red and gray squirrel."   September 28, 1891

A Patient Wife

December 19, 1898 - *Naples Record*

"Last Saturday, while Mrs. G.C. Greiner was going to North Cohocton the horse and cutter suddenly tipped over. Fortunately, a man happened along soon, unhitched the horses and tipped back the cutter, and found Mrs. Greiner patiently waiting. She says she had to take it cool, as the snow was about four feet deep and just her head stuck out.
(Alice Jane (Bartholomew) Greiner, was about 53 when this happened. She was the daughter of Aaron & Ann (Briggs) Bartholomew also of Garlinghouse)"

A Teacher

1897-1898 - Carlinville IL Daily Enquirer

DIVIDING THE PROFITS.

"The four-year rotation gives us another advantage; it divides our work more evenly all through the season. All the work of the rye crop comes at a time when the farmer has nothing driving to do. The sowing is done when the oat crop is out of the way and the potato or corn crop not yet ripe enough to require our attention. The harvesting also comes at a time when no other work is crowding, between haying and oat harvest. By dividing our acreage in this way, setting part of it aside for the rye crop, we have a better chance to do our spring seeding and planting with the necessary care and thoroughness.—G. C. Greiner, in Farm and Fireside."

January 7, 1898- The Pine Plains Register

FARM AND GARDEN - TYING A BRIDLE.

"Right and Wrong Way of Knotting Leather Straps. As I was driving under the shed of one of our stores recently, writes G. C. Greiner, I found there a team already hitched to the manger. One of the horses had slipped his bridle from its head and was trampling it in the dirt. After securing my own team, I also adjusted a dangling bridle to its proper place. Entering the store, I met the owner of the team, and in course of our conversation, I mentioned to him the condition of his horse as I found it.

"Well," he said, "no matter where and when you tie that horse he will either slip his bridle or untie the straps."

From a few points of arguments that were exchanged between us I found that my friend either did not know or never had tried the proper way of bridling a horse or tying a strap to the manger.

The throat-latch of his bridle hung far down, so loose that I had no trouble in slipping the bridle into the horse's head without unbuckling the same. A reverse action, caused by the horse rubbing his head against a post or manger, would of course allow the bridle to slip off again. It is the object of the throat-latch of halters and bridles to keep them securely in place, and if our friend had buckled It just loose enough so it would not choke the horse the bridle would never have come off. In tying the lead-strap to the manger the same mistake was made. The tie was too loosely made to be safe, and if the horse had any notion of nibbling at the strap he could easily untie himself.

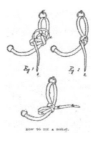

The illustration shows both the right and the wrong way of tying either leather straps or ropes. Fig. 1 is something like the tie referred to; it Is not reliable, although it may answer for a temporary hitch. But if I wanted to be positively sure that my horses could not get loose I would not stop short of the tie. Fig. 2. This is the same as Fig. 1, except that every part of it Is drawn up tight. To make it, tie the common bow-knot, Fig. 3, drawing the knot (a) fairly tight; pass the end (b) of the strap through the bow or loop (c), and draw the loop by pulling at strap (d) until it hugs the end (b). When doing this, the knot (a) is liable to loosen, which must be prevented by holding it with thumb and forefinger of one hand while the other does the pulling. Then draw the end (b) through the drawn-up loop (c), Fig. 2, as far as possible, and you will have a tie that no animal is able to undo."

Honey Business

August 18, 1886 - *Naples Record*

"G.C. Greiner has left us a sample of honey, and says the season is not a good one for its production owing to the drouth (sic) he will have a very light crop, and probably that will be the case with all in this section. He will have about two tons when he expected six."

The A B C and X Y Z of bee culture; a cyclopedia of everything pertaining to Honey Peddling
By Amos Ives Root, Rob Root (1919) Pg. 447 -
Another experience is thus given by G. C. Greiner of La Salle, N.Y.:

"Peddling honey has, like everything else, its ups and downs. We don't always strike it rich.

Some days it may seem like terribly steep uphill business, while other days the money may roll in by the handfuls. As an illustration, and a proof that the latter sentence is almost literally true, let me give you one day's experience.

Late last fall, I chanced to take a trip to Niagara Falls with the intention of making a display of my goods at the city market. At first things looked a little gloomy. Purchasers did not flock in as I had hoped, until after some minutes of patient waiting. One passing lady, in looking at my honey, asked, "Is your honey pure?" The reply I made must be imagined, for it would fill more space than the editor would be willing to allow. But let me emphasize—here is where the blabbing came in. In answering her question, I delivered a good half-hour lecture in less than two minutes, trying to convince her of the purity and all the good points of my honey. In the mean time, passing people had stopped to listen; and by the time my lady friend was ready to buy one of my quart cans I had quite a crowd around me. To cut the story short, for quite a few minutes I handed out cans, mostly quarts, as fast as I could make change (many of the purchasers promising to buy more the next time I attended the market, if the honey proved to be what I had recommended it to be.)

When the market closed at 11 a.m., I had a few cans left. With these I drove to main Street and tied my horse in front of one of the stores, where I had a little business to transact. A few minutes later, while I was conversing with the storekeeper inside, some one opened the door and inquired: "Hello! Where is this honey-man?"

After introducing myself he requested me to show him what I had to sell. It did not take very long to convince him that I carried the genuine article; and what pleased me still more was the fact that he ordered two cans to be left at the corner drugstore across the street.

When I delivered the cans they were closely scrutinized by the clerks and some other parties who happened to be present, and one of the clerks asked:

"What guarantee do we have that this is pure honey?"

Here another lecture-like conversation, too long to be repeated, took place, the substance of which may be concentrated in my reply:

"First, pure honey and my name and address are on every package; and second, back of this is the New York State law that prohibits all honey adulteration."

Before I left the place I sold two more cans to those other parties.

A great help in selling honey on the road is a proper traveling-outfit, which enables us to present our products in clean, neat and inviting appearance. I know from experience that at least one-fourth of my sales of honey can be traced back to this feature."

1915 *The Ekalaka Eagle* Montana
Conveniences For Moving Bees

"In the cold climates where bees are wintered out of doors it is sometimes advisable to cover several colonies with one shed and to move them nearer the residence. Difficulties naturally arise in doing this, but these may be solved by a plan conducted by **G.C. Greiner** of Niagara County, N.Y. Mr. Greiner has used a sled somewhat resembling a combined stone boat and sleigh. The runners are made of 3 by 5 scantlings and the platform of one inch stuff. To the runners is fastened a chain by means of clevices.

A carpenter's horse twelve inches high is placed at one end of the little shed containing the bees. A jack, shown at the opposite end, is used to raise the house until the horse can be placed under it. When so placed the jack is removed to the other end and the house raised there. Then the sled is pushed beneath the house, the jack and the horse are removed and the whole thing dragged over the snow wherever desired. In unloading the reverse process is practiced. By means of these tools Mr. Greiner is able to handle his bees without serious jarring. Preferably the work should not be done until after snowfall."

Drawing accompanying the above article.

THE "MUSIC CORE OF FARMERS"

Well, it sounded pretty far-fetched to me, when I first heard brother Luie's description "Music Core of Farmers". How could I ever, have doubted the plans of such an energetic and creative man, like Karl Gotthold Greiner?

1874 - *Ontario Repository and Messenger*

"—The whisky band music, was not as good as the Brass Band music, down the lake on Thursday. If there is ever another meeting of the Band Association, proper officers will be present to nip the music of the whisky Band on the start. The Bands of music were composed of gentlemen, every one.

In regard to the Band Picnic at Seneca Point Thursday, the Record says it was a success, but the rain of the early morning deterred many visitors from attending, and lessened the number of bands that intended to be present. The Naples Cornet, Richmond C, Rushville C. and Greiner's band, Naples, were present, and a few members from others. The playing was excellent, and while each vied in excellence it is difficult to give either preference—The grand climax was to see them all in an immense circle, facing to the centre, and hear "Hail Columbia" twice through.

This grand tournament, originated by M. C. Sutton and carried out by Beeman and the rest of the Naples Band is likely to be a permanent good thing; an organization—permanent—was effected which is denominated *The Ontario Cornet Band Association.*

Officers for the ensuing year were elected as follows: M. C Sutton, Naples, President. E. M. Beeman, Naples, Secretary. Vice Presidents, Charles Ward, Richmond; Clarence Smith, Naples; D. W. Beam, Canadice; G. C. Greiner, Naples; Henry B. Whitman, Rushville; Ed. Bond, North Bloomfield ; Mr. Singerland, Canandaigua, Frank Montgomery, Prattsburg ; John Hanna, Lima, and J. C. Cole, Geneva. The Association resolved to meet next year at the same place, and the President and officers were duly empowered to call the meeting at the proper time."

July 18, 1874

"Address G C. Greiner, Naples, if you wish the services of a good Cornet Band."

Oct. 1872 – Naples Record

"MR. EDITOR—I saw in the Record a notice of a pole raising to come off at Garling House being the first of the season, I had a little anxiety to be present, I started en-route for that place arriving in good time, every thing in readiness, capstand anchored &c., G. C. Greiner's Cornet Band stationed ready to strike in one of their patriotic strains at the word of command, hundreds of willing "hands ready with pikes and guys. At the word of command every one seemed anxious to do more than their part, the huge pole was seen to move steadily and surely as the voice of the captain was heard distinctly above the music. That being discoursed by the band, seemed to inspire each one with enthusiasm that burst forth from every one as soon as they saw the pole standing erect with the star-spangled-banner unfurled to the breeze waving so proudly over them. Messrs Daggart and Olney from Nunda mounted the platform and delivered each an address followed by our Hon. Assemblyman C. S. Lincoln. All this time the ladies was preparing the table which was groaning under the weight of goodies which looked so inviting to the hungry ones; presently after speaking the band took the lead under the direction of the Marshal of the day) and lead the procession to the table, it being a free dinner to all, all was invited to surround the table and was waited upon by the committee in a praiseworthy manner until all was satisfied. And the ladies know just how to get up a rousing dinner I should judge by the looks of the table full of pyramids together with an endless lot of cakes pies and many other things too numerous to mention. All passed of harmoniously and we had a pleasant time. A SPECTATOR."

December 7, 1927-*Cohocton Valley Times Index*
WEST COHOCTON

"…One day not long ago as I sat thinking about my school days when a boy the thought came to me in regard to the Garlinghouse brass band where I lived fifty-eight years ago, and since that time— oh how the 16 band boys have been dropping from the ranks one by one, until all are gone but three. The number 3 remaining today are Isaac Goundry, Mark Wright and Martin Lyon.

Charles Griener, a German, who lived with us was our instructor or leader and a good accomplished musician. While in those days this band was supposed to be ready to furnish good music at Fourth of July Celebration, Presidential campaigns or any other gatherings for miles around. The Garlinghouse brass band as they were called 58 years ago, always started the heel arocking with its melodies that filled the bill from start to finish wherever they went according to orders. Below I will give the names of the sixteen boys or young men that belonged to this brass band, from 1867 to 1874. Charles Greiner, Leader; Tuisco Greiner, Freedom Griener, Leonard Warner, Seymour Swarts, John Goundry, Isaac Goundry, James Frink, Chauncey Wright, Aaron Wright, Mark Wright, Iva Lyon, Martin Lyon, Frank Manahan, Riley Hancock, Eugene Briggs. Those still living are Isaac Goundry, Mark Wright and Martin Lyon."

(The author of this article was not noted)

For years, I wondered if Tuisco and Friedemann had played in the band with their brother, and finally, I happened on the answer when I wasn't even looking for it. I can almost imagine it – *how I wish I could have been there!*

Fifty-eight years ago from 1927 (the date on the article) puts the band formation at 1869 – the same year Gotthold returned from Germany on the S.S. Hansa with his brother Tuisco, and undoubtedly a wooden crate full of musical instruments, in the hold of the ship.

Chapter Seventeen

Getting to Know Friedemann Greiner

"Two skillful hands, with ten nimble fingers."

The Friedemann Greiner Family
Photo Courtesy Dave Olney – Friedemann's great-Grandson
Elsie, Harold, Friedemann, Sophia, Bertha

DONNA J. WELLS

The Friedemann Greiner Farm
Hunts Hollow Road, Naples, N.Y.

Photo Courtesy Dave Olney

"April 16, 1904 "This is now a pond and roadway moved down near apple tree. On Maple tree is father's bulletin board, "Honey for sale". This is my father's pear, plumb, peach and large chestnut orchards also cow pasture. The apple tree in middle of field is twenty-ounce. A neighbor Mark Washburn has team and bobs in roadway."

Sophia Greiner Olney

When I read this first couple of articles, and saw pictures of Friedemann, I imagined him to be a very serious man – as it turns out, I was wrong.

A Teacher & Research Scientist

BENDING SECTIONS

"(Written for the American Bee Journal by the late Friedemann Greiner, February 25, 1891.)"

"Mr. Englefeld wishes to know (page 265) whether anyone has a better way to dampen sections than his own. I think there is a better, or at least a much quicker way, to do it. Take a teapot filled with water and pour the water through the grooves before the sections are taken out of the crate. Within two minutes you can have a thousand sections ready to bend. But why dampen at all? Keep your sections in an underground room or place them in the cellar for a few days, and you will have a little trouble from broken sections. I seldom break more than one in 500. No machine is necessary for bending sections. Two skillful hands, with ten nimble fingers, can put them up at the rate of 1,000 per hour, as I have often done."

"Documents of the Assembly of the State of New York, Volume 21 by New York State Legislature, Assembly… Bureau of Farmers' Institutes Published 1902

Address at Bee-Keepers' Institute, Rochester, N.Y. pgs. 171-175
By F. Greiner, Naples, N.Y.
[Part of the bee-keepers present were not conversant with the English language, therefore the address was made in German.]

Mr. President and Bee-Keeping Friends. – There are a great many things *we think we know* which we really don't know at all. We only believe them, because some one in whom we have confidence has told us so. How few of us, for instance, have ever seen a queen bee lay eggs; caught her in the act. Yet we do not hesitate saying she does. Other similar things regarding the bee life we have only read in books or have some circumstantial evidence of, but real, positive knowledge of them we do not have. Of late years I have devoted considerable time to a study in which we who are here assembled are all interested, the study of the natural history of the bee. I will now proceed to tell you what observation I made on my glass hive.

The time chosen was during the warm days of August when the bees were at work on buckwheat. The hive contained four combs well filled with brood, was full of bees and had four glass sides. It stood by the window in my office, and the bees worked through under the slightly raised sash. I spent many hours, day and night, by the side of this hive waiting and watching for the development of certain things.... On August 1st a full-blood Italian queen had been introduced in place of the black, and commenced laying eggs on August 3rd. Watching on August 13th at 7 o'clock a.m., I discovered the queen on a comb next to the glass surrounded by eight or ten bees, all with their heads toward the queen. Within five minutes I saw the queen deposit six eggs in as many different cells. She would always examine a cell first before making preparations to deposit an egg in it. Traveling over the comb apparently in search of cells she occasionally paused and allowed herself to be fed by one or more of her attendant worker bees, which work, however did not occupy but a few moments at a time. The queen not only deposited eggs in worker cells, but also in drone cells. Each was marked as soon as the queen left the cell on the outside of the glass with pen and ink, and careful record was kept of all accompanying circumstances in a little book kept there lying on top of the hive.

Three days later the shells of the eggs bursted and tiny little worms (larvae) were born into the world. I could not see these very plainly without taking the comb out of the hive, which for some reasons I did not wish to do. During the following five or six days I watched the growth of these larvae. August 21st some of the worker larvae were being capped; at 10 o'clock p.m. some were fully sealed up and by morning of the next day all were sealed. It will be seen the time varied somewhat. A few larvae were being fed for five days and fourteen hours, others just six days…….

"My patience was somewhat tried waiting for the emerging of the matured drones. The books say they develop inside of twenty-four days, but it was not until September 6th at 11 o'clock p.m. that I saw the first one come to light, and a lamp light at that….

It has not yet been my good fortune to see a queen bee deposit an egg in a *queen cell*; when I do you may be rest assured I will watch with interest and anxiety how long it will take to bring a queen bee into the works under perfectly normal conditions."

"[NOTE. - The above is a somewhat condensed copy or translation of the original.]"

To be honest, my patience was somewhat tried, just reading this article. I left out an extensive mid-section of the article, myself – another highly detailed discussion of the age of the different classes of bees when they started doing the different tasks they were designed to accomplish during an average working life of "not much beyond forty days."

To someone who has a simple, non-technical mind – like I do, this article was fascinating, but at the same time, a little funny! Friedemann definitely was serious about his business… but he did have another side to him…

A Silly Sense of Humor

Sept. 17, 1913 – *Naples Record*

"The honey house in the Naples Grange exhibit was unique. It was from the apiary of Friedemann Greiner, who arranged the frame work with skeleton boxes and honey comb, and the bees did the rest. In the doorway stood a lady stylishly attired in a slit skirt. She was made by Mr. Greiner out of an inverted ear of corn with the husk on. A canoe in the Grange exhibit, made by Irving L. Kimber from a large cucumber, was also novel, especially after Mr. Greiner had added the finishing touches by making two Indians entirely out of vegetables and with heads of wheat for feathers on their heads, to ride the craft."

(Now I know where my mother got the silly gene... and it didn't stop there, either.)

Friedemann was clearly in awe of the natural wonders of creation. Like his brothers, he *couldn't* keep it to himself, he *had* to share it! How many of us might never have given another thought to the amazing things taking place around us everyday - everywhere we go - unless someone opened our eyes to them?

August 31, 1921 – *Naples Record*

"AN INVITATION The modern beehive may be compared to a book, which may be opened and the leaves examined, etc. This arrangement is an interesting one, both to the student of nature as well as to the practical honey producer. The student of nature may be interested in the life of the hornet as much as of the honey bee, and to such students I wish to extend an invitation to view a hornets' nest, attached to a window in one of our rooms, said hornets' nest offering an opportunity to observe from within, through the glass, the inmates building their nest, feeding and attending their young, etc. I invite the entomology class of Naples High School to come and see this wonder. An opportunity of this kind is rarely ever offered. F. Greiner."

A Perfectionist

January 16, 1901 – *The Naples Record*
From the Bee Keepers' Convention.
. . . .

"It is well understood that before fruit can set a grain of pollen from the anthors must reach the stigma of the blossom. This grain of pollen is not swallowed up, but, like a seed, germinates and sends its roots down to the ovaries or seedhouse of the blossom. If any bordeaux of paris green mixture has touched the stigma, pollen cannot germinate and fruit cannot set. The professor showed; in various ways how this was proven and that there can be no question but what spraying trees while in bloom is very unwise, resulting in a double loss—less fruit and injury to trees. The matter of honey adulteration received a great deal of attention, a few samples of adulterated honey in glass bottles which had been procured at stores in Geneva, were shown and sampled. It was conceded that there were no objections in selling any harmless mixtures of glucose in glass bottles if sold under their proper name; but objections were raised against selling them under the names of honey or maple syrup. On the statutes we have a law forbidding the selling of adulterated goods in disguise, but the State Board of Health has failed to enforce it. It was the opinion of all present that the enforcement of that law should be placed in the hands of the Commissioner of Agriculture, and a resolution to that effect was adopted… F. GREINER. NAPLES, N. Y., Jan. 12,1901."

1904 – *The Naples News*

"Naples takes a pride in her bee farmers and she has at least two of the best in the State. F. Greiner left with us yesterday a generous sample of his extracted honey which is par excellence in all the qualities of a perfect article. The flavor, body, transparency and color are all there. There are as many grades of extracted honey as of maple syrup. His is made of the complete, or "ripe" comb and is far more valuable than that extracted from unripe comb. Mr. Greiner says that this is an unusually good season for honey and this specimen is evidence of it. He has our hearty thanks."

The Hayseed - Defender of Common Sense

Concerning Watering Troughs:

August 14, 1902 – *Naples News*

"To the Highway Commissioner, the Supervisor, the Assesors: Public watering-troughs are none too many in the country. I could name several localities in this town that would be benefitted if good troughs were put in. Their erection should be encouraged rather than discouraged. Under the old system of road work a watering-trough counted three days for the owner and this in a measure was compensation for the trouble and expense to keep such a trough in repairs.

Some four or six years ago, when we changed to a money system, watering troughs were not taken into any account and the owners of such received no pay or privilege whatever during the two years the system was in force. On making inquiry I was informed that the Assessors had not made any provisions, and here the matter dropped.

We now have again changed to the money system (and I hope it may turn out more satisfactorily than it did the first time)." I inquired into the matter of watering-trough-recompensation again and find this: The assessors claim they can do nothing about it; the Supervisor makes the same claim. Who then has any authority to act?

I believe the public wants these troughs kept up, and more erected if possible. It is between the Highway Commissioner, the Supervisor and the Assesors that this matter lies. The assessors can as easily ascertain where there are good troughs as who keeps dogs. They could record the troughs, then the Supervisor would be in a position to adjust the tax accordingly.

Will anything be done?   August 11, 1902. F. Greiner."

TUISCO GREINER

Concerning Hitching Posts:

June 20, 1906 – *The Naples News*

"Editor of the NEWS. The Hayseeds are marveling, over the wisdom of the Fathers of our Village shown in their removal of the hitching posts which Main Street was once decorated with. The Hayseeds realize that a hitching post on a public street particularly in Naples in its present condition is a source of great danger. They may obstruct the path of the automobiles of which one is not always sure where it may land. The hitching post however has served the one good purpose of furnishing an anchor place for the team of the farmer while he is doing his trading at the stores. It cannot be denied that the farmers are becoming more and more independent of the town. They find it to their advantage to trade out of town. It saves valuable time. A load of goods may be brought from the depot in very much less time than it would require to (word unreadable) the purchase at the store in Naples nothing said about the saving of money. Our neighboring towns also furnish inducements in the way of hitching posts and free sheds, etc., which us ruralists appreciate. Undoubtly (sic) the promoters and executors of this wise measure, or otherwise, have taken all these conditions into consideration when the hitching posts were removed from the street without furnishing a more convenient and better place where teams could safely be left. It seems as plain as day that this one act of cutting down the hitching posts will do more toward driving the farmers out of town to do their trading in other places than anything that could have been done. Is the farmers trade worth anything to the town? Is it good policy to disregard their needs? These are questions to ponder over.

With due respect, one of the Hayseeds F. Greiner."

Concerning Road Repair:

April 21, 1915 – *The Naples Record*

"From Hunts Hollow -The weather has been ideal for drying out the roadbed we might have good traveling by this time if only the road commissioner had put in an appearance. We have noticed rather unimportant roads, like the Parrish cross road, below town, for instance, have been worked some time ago, presumably so that the Parrish cows might not stub their toes; but the Hunts Hollow highway first in importance as a road of travel, as a road that brings more produce to the Naples market than any other, over which very many autos travel every day and hour has been neglected, not only this spring but for over a year. It is full of holes and ruts and stones. The Hunts Hollow people wonder where the road commissioner is and what he is doing. Will we have to take it into our own hands and repair our roads? The taxpayers are considering the proposition."

F. Greiner. April 19, 1915.

Wonder how this one turned out…

May 13, 1914 – The Naples News

"Naples Grange will meet Saturday evening May 16th, at 7:30 p. m. Debate: Resolved that the wife should have equal share and voice with the husband in the use of family funds. Mrs. C. J. Smith Affirmative, **F. Greiner** Negative. Discussion: What fund producing resources should be under the wife's control for supplying the ever increasing demands of the household? Mrs. 0 A. Olney."

Chapter Eighteen

Tuisco, In Other's Words

"The previous writings of Mr. Greiner… have done so much to advance the gardening interests of the United States."

Canadian Horticulturist. Volume 24, 1901

"…At this stage of the proceedings my friend, Mr. T. Greiner, offered to take a hand and has been busy writing the following pages, which I take pleasure in presenting to the public as the very best and most practical work ever written for the benefit of the American vegetable gardener."

"…In this revised edition, I have little to add to the above remarks, further than that the unqualified endorsement and success of this work has far exceeded both Mr. Greiner's and my own highest expectations. Its cordial reception has encouraged us to make the second edition up to and abreast of these progressive times, and I can ask of my friends nothing more than this new revised edition of "How to Make the Garden Pay" shall receive as kind a reception as has been accorded the first edition of this work."

Yours Very Truly,

WM. HENRY MAULE.
January 15, 1895."

American Magazine, Christmas Issue 1912
Ad on page 104

HOW ABOUT THAT GARDEN?

"Have you that garden all laid out and planted yet? Well, there is still time. But the most important part is taking the right care of the garden after you have it planted. Thomas Greiner* who edits the Garden Department of FARM AND FIRESIDE, The National Farm Paper, is about the best authority on gardening anywhere. He has a large market garden near Buffalo and has made a big success of the business. Mr. Greiner, like all the rest of FARM AND FIRESIDE contributors, knows just what he is talking about, and stops when he is through. Besides gardening, this big farm paper treats on various phases of country life and farming. You will find it full of interesting articles, and stories that appeal to all members of the family. It will reach you every other Saturday. We guarantee that you will like it or your money back. For only fifty cents FARM AND FIRESIDE will be sent to you for a whole year, 26 big numbers. Order to-day. FARM AND FIRESIDE, SPRINGFIELD, OHIO"

*(aka Tuisco)

OUR BOOK TABLE - Canadian Horticulturist. Volume 24, 1901

Pg 259 - "A NEW BOOK ON GARDENING - The Farm Philadelphia, have just published a new book on gardening entitled, "The Garden Book for Practical Farmers" written by Mr. T. Greiner. Mr. Greiner has for thirty years been preaching and practicing the gospel of good gardening with marked success, and is well qualified for the task. Thirty years of actual soil contact by a man who loves his work and follows it in all its detail with indefatigable patience, means much when it comes to teaching others. In the garden book the author optimizes that thirty years' work in a most entertaining and instructive manner. The man who has a garden, large or small, and the man who intends to have one, will be equally interested and profited by a study of its pages. It is one of those books which inspires its readers to reach out for better results through more thorough work, and is in line with the previous writings of Mr. Greiner, which have done so much to advance the gardening interests of the United States. The book is handsomely printed in clear type on fine paper, containing 129 practical illustrations. The price is 50 cents, postpaid. It is right for every day reading and right for every day reference."

Who's Who In America. Vol. 2 1901-1902

Pg 463 - GREINER, Tuisco, agr'l editor; b. Bernburg, Germany, June 16, 1846; s. Karl and Carolina G.; academic ed'n Bernburg, Germany; m. 1st, Naples, NY., Hester Bartholomew, January 12, 1871; 2d, La Salle, N.Y., August 28, 1894, Cora E. Bartholomew. Engaged in writing on agriculture since 1880. Author: Money in Potatoes, 1882 O1; How to Make the Garden Pay, 1889 M24; New Onion Culture, 1890 A7; Practical Farm Chemistry, 1891 A7; Onions for Profit, 1892 B20; Celery for Profit, 1893 B20; Capons for Profit, 1894 A7; Young Market Gardener, 1896 A7; The Garden Book, 1901 F8

Chapter Nineteen

Goodbye... For Now

Tuisco & Cora

Elmlawn Cemetery, Buffalo, New York

Buried next to Cora is their son Paul, who was killed by a train. Daughter Helma would say he was the best behaved, and closest child to his mother - in life and now in death.

My mother, Betty June, could never bring herself to say good-bye. She would always say, "Good-bye... for now." She never knew her grandparents Tuisco and Cora Bartholomew Greiner. They both died 16 years before she was born. She would never meet her great Uncles Gotthold and Friedemann, who died only a few short years before her birth. She only knew their children, and grandchildren, and she spent happy days as a child visiting the Hunts Hollow Farm that meant so much to Tuisco and his brothers, each having lived there at one time or another.

Good-bye is hard to say even to someone you've never met – but I feel that I *have* met Tuisco Greiner, because of his books and articles - something I wish I could say about all of my ancestors. I am so grateful to have "heard" him speak from his heart the things that were important to him, the way he felt about his new country, his family, his garden, and the things that he enjoyed in his leisure time.

His obituary is fairly matter of fact – not as glowing as his more genial brother's. Perhaps because of his "tell it like it is" attitude, or perhaps because of "The Change". Perhaps there's another, more glowing obituary out there I have yet to find. Nevertheless, it is sad to reach the last chapter in the story of a remarkable man from a remarkable family. I am so grateful that he left so much of himself behind for us, his family - and for people all over the world who still value his wisdom, his unabashed love of the vegetable garden, and his wonderful, inspiring use of the pen.

Thank you great-Grandpa, you made a difference in my life.

Goodbye... for now.

April 11, 1914 - *Batavia Daily News, NY*

"Police Justice, Tuisco Greiner of La Salle was perhaps fatally injured yesterday when he fell and fractured his hip."

August 20, 1914 – *Naples Record*

"Tuisco Greiner and daughter, Helma, of LaSalle, at F. Greiner's."

September 15, 1914 North Tonawanda, N.Y., - *Evening News*

"Justice Greiner is critically ill.

Justice of the Peace Tuisco Greiner of La Salle, one of the best known men of the county, is critically ill with peritonitis at his home and no hope is held out of his recovery. Mr. Greiner, who has been justice of the peace for many years, recently was badly injured in a fall on the boulevard. His injuries were slow to heal and have aggravated his present malady."

September 20, 1914 - *Niagara Falls Gazette*
TUISCO GREINER, LA SALLE, DIES AT FALLS HOSPITAL
(Special Wire to The Courier.)

"Niagara Falls, Sept. 20 – Tuisco Greiner, peace justice at LaSalle, died at Memorial Hospital last night. Funeral will be held from his late residence on Creek road at 1 o'clock Tuesday afternoon. Burial will be in Elmlawn cemetery at Tonawanda.

Judge Greiner is survived by six children, Luis, Otto, Albin, Guido, Mrs. L. V. Luick (Zora), and Miss Helma Greiner. For some time Judge Greiner was in ill health and last Monday was operated on at the hospital. His wife died some time ago, following the tragic death of a young son, who was run down by a passenger train.

Deceased was born in Bernberg, Germany, June 16, 1846, and came to this country when twenty-three years old. He came to LaSalle in 1889."

September 30, 1914 -*Naples Record*

"Jesse Bartholomew, wife and nephew Guido Greiner and F Greiner and wife were called to La Salle, NY last Monday to attend the funeral of Tuisco Greiner, father of Guido and brother of F. Greiner."

September 23, 1914 – Naples Record

"Jesse Bartholomew and wife, Mrs. D. W. Briggs, and two children of the late Tuisco Greiner, who attended the funeral of Tuisco Greiner, in LaSalle, are expected home today."

Chapter Twenty

"An All-Abiding Faith"

(1913)

DEATH OF T. GREINER, OF LA SALLE, N. Y.

"We are just in receipt of a notice of friend Greiner's death, in a brief editorial in the Practical Farmer, for which he has been a valued writer for more than twenty years past. Our good friend has been a regular contributor to quite a number of our best journals on agriculture, horticulture, gardening, etc., almost all his life. His articles have not only been exceedingly practical, but every sentence and line indicated that he was in close touch with the soil every day of his life. His brother Fr. Greiner, has been a frequent contributor to our columns, and I think Tuscio (sic) will be found on pages 483, 568, and 656 for the present year. He and I have had frequent friendly letters for year past—in fact, almost ever since GLEANINGS was started. At first we did not agree very well on religious matters; but as friend Greiner was an ardent friend of temperance we soon got on common ground, and our relations in later years past have been of the most friendly nature. You can imagine how surprised and pained I was to receive last summer the following brief notice. I think there had to have been some correspondence previous to this in regard to this accident.

Mr. Root:—Radiograph taken of my damaged hip this week shows that I am hurt beyond repair, and shall never be able again to walk naturally or resume my garden work."

T. Greiner La Salle, N. Y., July 25

"On the same day the above was received I wrote him as follows:

Now, in regard to your sad condition. I hope it is only that you are unable to walk, and that you have all your other faculties. If so, you can still praise God. I am sure inventive Geniuses can furnish you something that will enable you to get around so you can at least oversee your garden work, and may be you can do it still better if you have more time to plan and arrange things. I suppose you know what Terry said when he was laid up one summer. He said he sat around under the shade trees and made the most profitable season he ever had, just by planning and bossing better. If you have any means in your place for storing an electric automobile I would suggest a little one as the best thing in the world to get around with. I use mine for running all over town, all over the farm, from my home to the factory, and everywhere I want to go; and it's really a Godsend to me to keep from getting too tired in walking.

May God help you in your affliction."

Medina, O., July 27.   A.I. Root.

Almost immediately I received the following:

"*Mr. A. I. Root:*—I thank you from all my heart for the kind letter of July 27, just received your kind and comforting words. I have much to be thankful for, with all my afflictions, for I have all my mental faculties and bodily health, except that break in my one hip bone, and have not missed nor failed to enjoy a meal for many months, perhaps years. I still hope to be of some use and usefulless to some one in this world, and to the world at large., and have an all-abiding faith in the hereafter.

I would thank you for a little more information about that small electric automobile. Who makes them, and what is the approximate cost? I have often wondered why somebody does not make and put on the market a low, small, safe vehicle of this kind calculated for a single passenger."

LaSalle, N.Y., July 29   T. Greiner

"As I did not know just how he stood in regard to spiritual matters you may imagine how rejoiced I was to hear him say, "I have an all-abiding faith in the hereafter." I hunted up a second-hand automobile, something like my own; but I presume his declining health prevented him from getting it. May God grant that we, each and all, may be able to say, before we cross the dark river that we "have an all-abiding faith in the hereafter."

A. I. Root of Gleanings in Bee Culture, Volume 42, pages 874-875

Chapter Twenty-One

The Name

I can't end the book without addressing the origins of the name, Tuisco. You would think that Tuisco Greiner was the only one in the whole world with that name, and I thought that was a fair statement until I did more research.

Soon after Tuisco arrived in 1869, there were, according to the 1870 U.S. census records, a Tuesco in St. Louis, Missouri, two Tuisko's, one in in San Franscisco, and one in Philadelphia and even a female named Tuiska in Cincinnati, OH. Other than that, there were many less similar names in the US, but no Tuisco's. There were however, many Tuisco's in Germany.

I decided that an online search was in order, to see if I could discover the origin of this unusual name "Tuisco".

This is what I found:

Politics and Reformations: Histories and Reformations – Essays in Honor of Thomas A. Brady, Jr.
Copyright 2007

"…but Franck begins from the earliest point possible, the German's origin. He argues that, 'we [Germans] do not come from a foreign people but from Tuisco, Noah's son. In this way, we fell in the land, procreated, and gave birth. Therefore, this is the origin of the land of Germany and of the Germans.' He confirms and legitimates this assertion on the widely-accepted authority of Tacitus. Franck also identifies Tuisco as the eponymous founder of the Germans, arguing that "they were named Germans (Teutsche), from Tuisco, son of Noah, just as the Romans traced their origins to Romulus and how the Christians were named 'Christian' from Christ…

…Franck argues that the Germans are both the descendants of Noah's son, Tuisco, and thereby indigenous, and Roman imperial heirs. He enhances the identity by arguing their culture is as rich and vibrant as that of the Greeks and Romans…"

…"The Tuisco mythology that the majority of German humanists utilized was Berosus' account. He argued that Noah was the father of the new age. Prior to the Flood, he fathered three sons, Shem, Ham and Japheth, and after it, he had many more sons, among whom the first*, was Tuisco. For an in-depth explanation of Tuisco and how the German humanists created the Tuisco mythology, see Munkler and Grunberger, "Origo et Vetustas," in Munkler, Grunberger and Mayer, Nationenbildung, pp. 246-61"

*Other accounts would say fourth and fifth son of Noah.

Tacitus:

Publius (aka Gaius) Cornelius Tacitus was an ancient Roman orator and historian born Ad 56 – a short time after Jesus was on earth. Tacitus was considered the greatest historian writing in the Latin language.

He writes:

"In ancient lays, their only type of historical tradition, they celebrate Tuisto, a god brought forth from the earth. They attribute to him a son, Mannus, the source and founder of their people, and to Mannus three sons… Some people, inasmuch as antiquity gives free reign to speculation, maintain that there were more sons born from the god and hence more tribal designations- Marsi, Gambrivii, Suebi, and Vandili-and that those names are genuine and ancient." (2.2)

Tuisco Greiner's ancestor is known to be Suebi, or Swabian. His ancestor, the original Greiner immigrant to Lauscha, Germany, was called Schwabenhans Greiner, meaning "Hans the Swabian".

There are other versions that have been considered – including Tuisto/Tuisco as a mythological giant, or that Tuisco was actually Ashkenaz, a descendant of Noah through his son Japheth, where the designation "Ashkenazi Jews" originated. (Jews that settled in Germany including an area in France originally part of Germany). Whatever the origins, "Tuisco" was, it seems, the god of Germany to ancient peoples who worshiped him.

Chapter Twenty-Two

Still Relevant

"Talent alone cannot make a writer. There must be a man behind the book."

Ralph Waldo Emerson

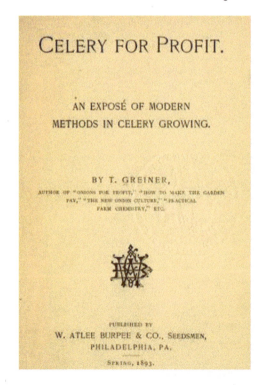

Tuisco's books are still valued for their timeless wisdom and are being reprinted and sold on numerous shopping websites including Amazon and ebay. They are listed for sale in numerous countries all over the world. They can also be read for free on books.google.com.

The books are listed in the catalogs of major Libraries and Universities, including the USDA National Agricultural Library.

The following statement by "Scholar's Choice," * is found on readings.com and other websites such as Amazon.com, in reference to historic books, including those written by Tuisco Greiner;

"This work has been selected by scholars as being culturally important, and is part of the knowledge base of civilization as we know it.... this work is important enough to be preserved, reproduced, and made generally available to the public. We appreciate your support of the preservation process, and thank you for being an important part of keeping this knowledge alive and relevant."

*(Not affiliated with book publishers of the same name in Rochester, NY.)

Authors of books and articles on vegetable gardening still value Tuisco's work and are "keeping this knowledge alive and relevant." They quote him in their own gardening publications:

"The Four Season Farm Gardener's Cookbook"
by Barbara Damrosch and Eliot Coleman (2012)

Pg. 14 - "As Tuisco Greiner, a 19th-century garden writer said in the delightful prose of his day, 'But it is with soils as it is with people when they get into a bad way. If the foundation – the texture, the quality, the character - is good, they can be redeemed very easily.'"

Heirloom Celery Varieties
by William Woys Weaver in motherearthnews.com,
April 24, 2012

"Tuisco Greiner, author of How to Make the Garden Pay, produced a small manual in 1893 called Celery for Profit, distributed by W. Atlee Burpee. Greiner was himself an upstate New York celery grower, and his book is full of interesting facts about varieties from that period. It is still a useful guide on celery cultivation today, especially for kitchen gardeners interested in raising heirloom sorts on a small scale."

UC Master Gardeners of Monterey Bay – Home Gardening Tips

by Paul McCollum (2013) ucanr.edu/blogcore
Regarding the Olive Squash;

"…Tuisco Greiner (1890, 257) listed it as a variety recommended for kitchen gardens. Its popularity in this country has been mixed, doubtless due to competition from so many other squashes better suited to our cookery. Perhaps it is just the dull color of the skin that Americans are not accustomed to, yet each squash yields an abundance of beautiful, thick, yellow flesh that is both sweet and flavorful. It makes excellent puddings and preserves… Greiner was correct in recommending this variety for small gardens because the vines trail close to the ground and are not long and tangled like the Hubbard."

Skill Cult – Land Alchemy
skillcult.com/blog

"The Historic Potato Onion: A compilation of early references."

Blog writer quotes an entire section from Chapter Ten of Tuisco's "The New Onion Culture: a complete guide in growing onions for profit", which gives information and instructions on growing the potato onion."

TUISCO GREINER

Publications by Tuisco Greiner

Money in Potatoes – 400 Bushels to the Acre as a Field Crop - 1882
Garden Talks magazine – 1883
How to Grow Onions; With Notes on Varieties – 1888*
(T. Greiner, New Jersey & Col. C. H. Arlie, Oregon)
How to Make the Garden Pay - 1890
Practical Farm Chemistry: A Handbook of Profitable Crop Feeding – 1891
Celery for Profit –1893
Onions for Profit –- 1893
Wood Ashes and their use. - 1894
The Young Market Gardener: Beginner's Guide – 1896
The New Onion Culture – a Story of Gardeners Young and Old - 1896
The Garden Book for Practical Farmers – 1901
The New Onion Culture: A Complete Guide in Growing Onions for Profit – 1903 and 1916
Capons for Profit – 1903

Note: These publications are still read and quoted by garden enthusiasts today. They can be read on googlebooks.com, and reprints and originals can be purchased on amazon.com and other websites. I add this information, because I value my great-grandfather's still timely and wise advice, although I have no connection to the publishers that are reprinting his works, and do not personally benefit in any way, by mentioning it here.

1992 Schott's Glass Employee Article

Source: Schott Intern – 4/1992 - Schott Glas - Mainz, Germany
Mainzer Schott employee, Jeffrey Wells looking for ancestors.

"Many Schott employees see him every day but few know his name, Jeffrey Wells. He has been working at Schott Glass Works Mainz since 1986 but only found out a few years ago what kind of special connection he has to Schott and that for many generations, to be more specific since 1597.

Jeffrey Wells has brown, wide awake eyes, a short-trimmed beard and speaks Mainz slang with an American accent. "Dreffen wir uns um vertel nach vier" (shall we meet at a quarter past four) he suggests which, is when his shift at the main gate at Hattenbergstrasse ends. He has collected stacks of files, old books, copies and many papers of translations. Genealogy has been his hobby for the past three years.

Jeffrey Wells was born Sept. 13, 1959 in Canandaigua New York. The trigger for his research was his Grandmother Helma a born Greiner. She was born in La Salle better known today as Niagara Falls. She told him the stories of the forefathers. This was a family saga which Jeffrey didn't know about when he started working at Schott, but that's the irony of life, because the Greiner clan was working with glass for many years. The oldest ancestor found is the Schwabe Hans Greiner. He moved to Thuringia in 1595 and settled in Lauscha. Two years later he and his friend Christoph Müller (Mueller) built the first glasshut in Thuringia. In Lauscha, Jeff was able to fill many blank spots in his family chronic. In 1997 – the 400th anniversary – the small town in Thuringia wants to honor Hans Greiner which is late recognition of probably the most famous son of Lauscha. The next highlight of Wells' gallery of ancestors is – Gotthelf Greiner – from Limbach, Germany - born in 1732. He is recognized as the inventor of the Thuringia porcelain. As proof Jeffrey Wells has a copy of the ancient piece: a play from 1859 which graphically represents Gotthelf Greiner's life.

The original biography still has not been found. Genealogy! The life of the Greiner family stretches through many pages and branches through the centuries. Son, grandchildren, great-, great-, great-, great-, great-, great-, great-, great-, great-, great-, great-, great-grandfather, Hans Greiner. Uh! Hundreds of names in a row left and right, up and down. The fate in which they were bound to could only be imagined. Paul T. found on one page "killed by train. March 12, 1912". Many different occupations are represented: musicians, director of a sugar refinery and of course many, many glassmakers. Ernst Friedrich Ferdinand Greiner born 1768 is believed to even have apprenticed as salesman at Scheirmann in Mainz. On the other hand, according to a document from April 22, 1532, we find connections to ancestors of the Schott family. In-between are missing pieces. Jeffrey Wells: "We have many old German books which my wife has translated in English. But some dates were unreadable, some pages missing". Eventually his great-grandfather, Tuisco Greiner appears. He was born June 16, 1846 in Bernburg (Thuringia): he died Sept. 19, 1914 in America. He was able to find out that Tuisco worked at the post office. Apparently, he had difficulties with his boss. Either way he migrated to America. In the United States, he became an author and wrote several books about gardening.

Jeffrey Wells is anxious to fill the blank spots. "The main thing I want to find out is when my greatgrandfather left Germany for America". The last traces lead to Bernburg. "Schott Intern" will participate in the search. We would be thankful for any information leading to the answer.

Footnote: Jeffrey Wells's genealogy is a story which life wrote. In 1945 the US Army made it possible for Erich Schott and his closest employees to leave Jena and escape the Soviets in the "train of the 41 glassmakers". Without the US Army, the Schott group in the west wouldn't have developed the way we know it now. Jeffrey

Wells joined the US Army in 1977 and transferred to Mainz two years later. He was stationed at Lee Barracks 4/69 Armor Battalion. Without the US Army Jeffrey would never have come to Germany where he met his wife, without his wife he wouldn't have stayed in Mainz, without the Army he wouldn't have come to Schott, without Schott Jeffrey Wells wouldn't have started his genealogy, without Jeffrey Wells everybody would drive through the main gate without permission and without Jeffrey Wells we would have never heard this beautiful story.

The original German article was written by Michael Bonewitz (Schott Intern – 4/1992)"

An Unforgettable Greiner Reunion

Newspaper Article shared by Anke Mieth, a Greiner Cousin who was instrumental in making this reunion a happy reality.

Greiner cousins representing countries from all over the world met for the first time in Lauscha, Greiner homeland in The Thuringian Mountains. We found each other on the Facebook page, "Descendants of Schwabenhans Greiner" created by Jeffrey H. Wells. I am so grateful that Jeff and I could be there to share in this amazing "reunion"!

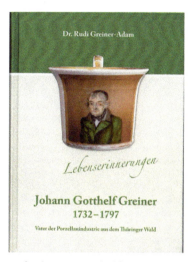

Memoirs of Johann Gotthelf Greiner 1732-1797
"Father of the Porcelain Industry from the Thuringian Forest"
By Dr. Rudi Griener-Adam

    Thank you, distant cousin Rudi, for giving us so much more of our Greiner family history than we ever imagined possible, and for immortalizing the family tree in your book, and on a wall of the Greiner room in the Otto Ludwig Museum in Eisfeld, Germany!

Distant Cousins

Rudi and Sigrid Greiner-Adam with my brother, Jeffrey H. Wells

Article

A Lovely Ending in a Shady Grove

"Come to me all you who are weary and burdened and I will give you rest."

Matthew 11:28

September 14th, 1872 - *The Naples Record*

PIC-NIC AT HICKORY BOTTOM.— The Sabbath school and day school, taught by Mrs. Alice Manahan held a social Pic-nic last Friday in a beautiful grove on Mr. Horace Gillet's farm. The day was pleasant and the whole neighborhood came out with their best productions, that was inviting to see, and to taste. H. A. Goodrich, was made President and L. M. Anable, Esq. Marshal of the day with W. T. Manahan Asst.

A large choir, in the best of practice, made excellent music from choice selection pieces, and it was reserved for the Garlinghouse Brass Band under their leader Mr. Griner (Gotthold) to fill out the programme of music in their best style, and the pleasing rolling strain played upon the snair drum by the unrivaled player, Martin Lyon, was among the best of the entertainment.

Good speeches "were made by Rev. W. B. H. Beach, S. H. Sutton and S. C. Lyon, spicy in anecdote, and happy illustrative, encouraging to the young and applauded by the old, to progress in all the moral, practical, useful, pursuits of life.

For one hour and a half the audience were delighted with the singing the speeches and the band, and were then marched away to the three long tables that shone resplendent with the rich delicacies of roast meats, sweetmeats, substantials, pyramids, and large cakes, beautifully decorated—some having political insignia suggestive of the Presidential Candidates interspersed with boquets of richest flowers—and the large committee of young ladies, smilingly served all from the rich laden tables, and the feast was still prolonged by the arrival of a full supply of delicious peaches by Mrs. E. G. Washburn.

The good ladies of Hickory Bottom had done their best. The farmers and their families had forgotten (sic) the toils of a long hot summer and each and all enjoyed this God-made institution of sociablity, of friendship, and rest made sweet by music, speech, and song.

The young were, instructed and the old were rejuvenated; a motion was carried to hold a pic-nic here in one year from to-day.

Index of Names

Counties in New York State covered: Monroe, Niagara, Ontario, Steuben, Yates
Other Locations covered: Germany, Red Bank, NJ, Richmond, VA,

A

Allen, (Superintendent)
Anable, L. M.

B

Bailey, Charles
Bartholomew, Aaron (A.)
Bartholomew, Angeline
Bartholomew, Ann
Bartholomew, Cora
Bartholomew, David
Bartholomew, Jesse
Bartholomew, John
Bartholomew, Perry
Bartholomew, William, Wm. (father)
Bartholomew, William, Wm. (son)
Barnes, Charles
Beach, Rev. W. B. H.
Beahan, Dr.
Beeman, E.M.
Beam, D.W.
Boles, Sam
Bond, Ed.
Bogart, Belmont D.
Bogart, Humphrey D.
Bogart, Maude
Bowen, E.P.
Briggs, Elwin
Briggs, Eugene
Briggs, Georgia (nee Greiner)
Briggs, Grace (nee Bartholomew)
Briggs, Jennie
Briggs, Lillian
Brooks, Fred
Brophy, Thomas
Brown, Waldo P.

C

Cannon, Joseph
Cannon, William
Cary, Mr.
Case, Stuart (Casey)
Caulkins Bro's
Caulkins, Hattie
Chormann, Frederick
Clark, E.C.

Clason, Rome
Coburn, F.D.
Cole, J.C.
Cramer, F.G.
Cristel, Uncle

D

Dadant, Mr.
Daggert, Mr
Davis, E.S.
Deyo, G.C.
Doppelmair, Captain
G. of Kiev, Russia
Dudley, Frank A.

E

Earle, President

F

Falconer, Wm.
Farrier Place NJ
Fees, Frank
Fisher, Wilson
Franz, Walter
Freeman, Harry
French, Ben
Frink, F.H.
Frink, James

G

Garlinghouse, Benjamin
Garlinghouse, Caroline
Garlinghouse, James
Garlinghouse, John
Gillette, Assemblyman
Gillette, Horace
Gombert, William

Goodrich, Carl (Karl)
Goodrich, Carrie (nee Greiner)
Goodrich, H. A.
Goodrich, Mortimer
Gorbachev, Mr.
Gordon, G.A.
Gould, John
Goundry, Isaac
Goundry, John
Granby Bro's.
Granby, Chas. L.
Gray, George
Greenwaldt, George
Greiner, Albin
Greiner-Mai, Albrecht
Greiner, Alice Jane (nee Bartholomew)
Greiner, Alice (Allie)
Greiner, August Ludwig
Greiner, Bertha (nee Jennings)
Greiner, Bessie
Greiner, Caroline (nee Naeter)
Greiner, Catherine
Greiner, Charlie
Greiner, Cora (nee Bartholomew)
Greiner, Graf Eberhardt der (Count Eberhard the Cantankerous)
Greiner, Ernst Friedrich Ferdinand
Greiner, Florine
Greiner, Friedemann
Greiner, Gotthold, aka Charles, G.C., C.G.
Greiner, Guido, Sr.
Greiner, Harriet (nee Wells)
Greiner, Hans "Schwabenhans"
Greiner, Harold (father)

Greiner, Harold Frederick (son)
Greiner, Helma (Greiner Bro's sister)
Greiner, Hester (nee Bartholomew)
Greiner, Hilmar
Greiner, Johann Gotthelf
Greiner, Jose Luis
Greiner, Joseph (Tuisco)
Greiner, Karl Justus
Greiner, Leo (Germany)
Greiner, Lieutenant
Greiner, Luie (Louis)
Greiner, Mary E.
Greiner, Otto (Tuisco's brother)
Greiner, Otto (Tuisco's son)
Greiner, Paul (Ludwig's son)
Greiner, Paul (Tuisco & Cora's son)
Greiner-Adam, Rudi
Greiner-Adam, Sigrid
Grose, Albert L.

H

Hale, Hon. J.H.
Hanna, John
Hancock, Riley
Harding, Joseph (Tuisco)
Hartmann, Fred
Hatch, Z. Paten
Hennig, (writer)
Hepburn, Katherine
Herzog, Professor
Hinkley, Edwin
Hoffman, J.
Hopkins, President
Houghtalin, James
Housel, H.A., Henry
Hunt, Aaron T.
Hunt, Elanor

J

Jayne, Dr.
Johnson, B.F.
Jones, Edward A.
Jordan Bro's

K

Kayner, Albert
Kellogg, Dr. J.H.
Kelly, J.W.H.
Kimber, Irving L.
Kinsey, H.C.
Knight, Frank

L

Landrigan, John A.
Leggett, John H.
Legore, John
Lewis, Frank
Liddiard, D.W.
Lincoln, Hon. C.S.
Lincoln, Wm. E.
Long, Elias A.
Lovett, John T.
Luick, Zora (nee Greiner)
Lyon, Iva
Lyon, Martin
Lyon, S. C.

M

Manahan, Alice
Manahan, Frank
Manahan, W. T.
Marks, Wm.
Marshall, Esq.
Masten, Rev. J.H.

McFarland, Mr.
McMahon, Douglas
McMahon, Reginald
Merrill, Cornelia (nee Scott)
Merrill, Helma (nee Greiner)
Merrill, Monique Marcelle Francette (nee Monnot)
Merrill, Raymond Briggs
Merrill, Raymond Greiner "Bud"
Merrill, Sidney Jerome, S.J.
Merritt, A.H.
Miner, Charles
Montgomery, Frank
Moulton, H.
Müeller, Christoph

N

Naeter, Ernst Friedrich
Newman, Thos. G.

O

Oehlmann, Fritz
Oehlman, William
Olney, Dave
Olney, Mrs. H. Warren
Olney, Mrs. O. A.
Olney, Sophia (nee Greiner)

P

Parcelly, Rev. D.A.
Parker, Dr.
Partington, Rev. William
Peck, Hiram (Sherriff)
Pickel, Miss Mathilda
Pottle, F.M.
Pulver, Elizabeth (nee Bartholomew)

R

Reagan, Ronald (President)
Reed & Pottle
Reichert, Edward
Reichert, George
Reinhardt, Auguste
Rosenthal (Locksmith)

S

Shaw, Mrs. H.E. (nee Elsie Greiner)
Singlerland, Mr.
Smith, Clarence
Smith, Coroner
Smith, Mrs. C. J.
Spagnolia, Anthony
Spalding, D. Gurney
Stahl, John M.
Stewart, Henry
Strassburg, Ferdinand
Sullivan, Mr.
Sutton, M.C.
Sutton, Myron
Sutton, S. H.
Swartz, Seymour

T

Terry, T.B
Tompkins, H.S.
Torrey, H.H.
Tryniski, Tom

W

Waite, D.B.
Walbridge, Orson
Ward, Charles
Warner, Leonard

Warner, Rev.
Washburn, Mrs. E. G.
Watkins, Flora (nee Bartholomew)
Weber, Heirich
Weld, Eber
Wells, Claudia (nee Göbig)
Wells, Jeffery H.
Wemette, Rev. F.L.
Westbrook, Nellis
Wheeler, Seymour
Whitman, Henry B.
Whitman, H.C.
Williams, E.T.
Williams, I.C.
Wilson, Galen
Wohlschlagel, Mr.
Wren, John (Detective)
Wright, Aaron
Wright, Chauncey
Wright, David
Wright, Harold Bell
Wright, Mark

About the Author

Donna J. Wells grew up in the beautiful heart of the Finger Lakes, where her ancestors settled (many of them soon after the American Revolution). She and her family had the unusual opportunity to live in both maternal and paternal grandparents' homes. Most of her childhood was spent at the Wells home farm in Honeoye Falls, New York, then, at the age of fourteen, the family moved into the Merrill family home farm in Naples, New York. Both homes had attics, drawers, closets, and cellars full of family heirlooms and pictures—a treasure trove that ignited a love of family history in Donna's heart.

The move came at a tumultuous time for the family, and Donna did not adjust well to the change. She was, in some ways, like her great-grandfather, Tuisco Greiner. She was opinionated, strong-willed, and rebellious—often mixed up in trouble. At nineteen, she took a bus to Los Angeles, thinking she would become a singer. Instead, she became a single mother, and everything changed. Family became very important to her. She wanted her daughter to grow up knowing the love of God and family, so she brought the baby home, to the family farm in Naples.

Eventually, Donna moved away from Naples, working in customer service for many years. She's now a self-employed writer and helps others find the joy of family history with her business, "Letter from Home Genealogy". She also enjoys spending time with her family in Naples and with her daughter, who is now happily married, and has three tall and handsome teenage sons!

CPSIA information can be obtained
at www.ICGtesting.com
Printed in the USA
BVHW02s0102010918
525581BV00003B/2/P